P9-CMW-322

# Advice for Dancers

# Advice for Dancers

## Emotional Counsel and Practical Strategies

Linda H. Hamilton, Ph.D.

Jossey-Bass Publishers
San Francisco

Substantial discounts on bulk quantities of Jossey-Bass books are available to corporations, professional associations, and other organizations. For details and discount information, contact the special sales department at Jossey-Bass Inc., Publishers (415) 433-1740; Fax (800) 605-2665.

For sales outside the United States, please contact your local Simon & Schuster International Office.

www.josseybass.com

TCF   Manufactured in the United States of America on Lyons Falls Turin Book. This paper is acid-free and 100 percent totally chlorine-free.

Sargent's weight/height table reprinted by permission of American Society for Clinical Nutrition from Sargent, D. W. (1963). Weight-Height Relationship of Young Men and Women. *American Journal of Clinical Nutrition, 13,* 318–325.

**Library of Congress Cataloging-in-Publication Data**

Hamilton, Linda H.
    Advice for dancers : emotional counsel and practical strategies /
Linda H. Hamilton. — 1st ed.
      p.  cm.
    Includes bibliographical references (p.   ) and index.
    ISBN 0-7879-4043-7 (alk. paper)
      1. Dance—Psychological aspects.  2. Dance—Vocational guidance.
I. Title.
GV1588.5.H35   1998
796.72—dc21                           .           98–10644

FIRST EDITION
*HB Printing*   10 9 8 7 6 5 4 3 2 1

# Contents

Introduction                                                        1

1. Accepting the Dancer You Are                                     9

2. Teaching Practices: The Good, the Bad, the Ugly                 35

3. Focusing on Body Shape and Appearance                          55

4. Your Relationships: Friends or Foes?                            77

5. So You Want to Be a Professional                                99

6. Performing at Your Peak                                        123

7. The Mind-Body Connection:
   Injuries and Your Health                                       147

8. Is There Life After Dance?                                     173

Resource Directory                                               193

Bibliography                                                     213

Further Reading                                                 217

About the Author                                                219

Index                                                          221

*This book is dedicated with heartfelt love and affection to my husband William G. Hamilton, M.D. His love, constant support, and own exemplary work as an orthopedic surgeon in dance medicine have been a shining light in my transition from dance to my new career in clinical psychology.*

# Advice for Dancers

# *I*ntroduction

*D*ancing is a way of life. From daily class to the heady pursuit of artistic perfection, dancers exist in a perpetual state of learning, reaching beyond personal limitations to realize their potential. A dancer's work, like a garden, is never completed but always growing. At its best, it transcends ordinary experience by expressing an essential part of our being through movement. We enter another realm filled with joy, exhilaration, and rapture.

Being a dancer is a wonderful experience. Yet there's a downside to this single-minded pursuit, when injuries, eating disorders, unemployment, and other forms of occupational stress take their toll. Because dancers rarely complain, many people believe that they live on air, forsaking food, money, and financial security all for the sake of their muse. The truth is that dancers are human. Over time, the joy of dancing is often lost, and hardship comes to dominate this existence. Admired for their stoicism, is it any wonder that dancers keep their problems to themselves?

In the past, the dance world encouraged us to be silent in the face of problems. Breaking this silence takes courage. Certain subjects have been traditionally off-limits, such as abusive teaching practices or sexual harassment. Yet the time has come to give dancers a voice rather than letting them deal alone with their worries.

I know about dancers, because I have danced for most of my life. At age eight I entered the School of American Ballet and went on to perform with the New York City Ballet under George Balanchine for nineteen years. Now I work as a clinical psychologist specializing in the performing arts, but I speak for the dancer I once was, as well as for the thousands whom I hear from monthly through my advice column in *Dance Magazine*. Yes, dancers can speak—and they have a lot to say about how they are treated and what they hope to accomplish in dance. After years of deafening silence, I believe that it's time to take their concerns to heart.

Dancers are special people. They care about dancing not with the calculated concern for a career but with the passion of a religious vocation. They are willing to push past the point of exhaustion in order to achieve their goals. In this way, dancers are like other dedicated athletes and artists who embark on a mission to be their best. Each day is a challenge that requires sweating it out in class and putting up with sore muscles and blisters. I can understand the obsession. Dancing was my first love, too.

According to my mother, I decided to dance before the age of five. Looking back at that child now, I wish that she had been better prepared to navigate the various conflicts and obstacles one faces in this career. Nothing is as difficult as dance or, paradoxically, as satisfying when all goes well. Unfortunately, most dancers hit a roadblock at some point, whether it is thwarted aspirations, unemployment, weight, or injuries. Hard work will only take you so far in dance; you also need to know how to avoid all the pitfalls along the way.

As a dancer, I experienced the joys and sorrows of dance firsthand: the elation of performing, the despair of being injured, the need for approval—all were frequent if unlikely companions. And when an early marriage to a musician failed, my husband asked me to see a psychologist before seeking a divorce. The intensity of the sessions, with their focus on self-expression and personal growth, reminded me of the stage. Surprisingly, therapy offered solutions to many of my problems, though not my marriage. These experiences motivated and inspired me to study psychology with a focus on the performing arts while I was still dancing. For eight years, I attended college and graduate school full time. I would do my homework in the dressing room at Lincoln Center, run to my academic classes between rehearsals, then race back to the theater to put on my makeup for the evening performance. When touring in other cities in the United States, I would sleep on planes in order to return to school on my only day off from dance. When I performed abroad, my mother sat in on classes and took notes.

During this period, I also became involved in doing research on occupational stress in dancers from America, China, Russia, and Western Europe. My dissertation focused on the joys and the pitfalls of performing, both of which affect self-esteem. After I became a licensed clinical psychologist, I discovered that there was no one else like me talking about a formal proficiency in performance psychology.

I began to treat a broad spectrum of dancers of all ages and levels, gaining greater knowledge through this experience, while continuing my research on performers. This, in turn, lead to my writing a psychological advice column in *Dance Magazine*. As a columnist, I heard from older and younger dancers from all walks of life, their families, and their teachers. This interaction provided even more experience, data, and interaction with the various problems that dancers face.

Today I consult, lecture, and counsel dancers in my private practice, as well as at the School of American Ballet and the Alvin Ailey American Dance Center. My understanding of the survival skills necessary in dance led to my writing this book, intended for all dancers everywhere.

Changes are occurring in the dance community. Over the past twenty-five years, dance medicine has emerged as a unique subspecialty of performing arts medicine, with textbooks, articles, and conferences geared toward dancers' needs. The approach to dance medicine is interdisciplinary in nature, because dancers—like other athletes—suffer from a wide range of orthopedic, hormonal, nutritional, and psychological problems. Specialists in each of these areas exist, as well as thirty-five clinics throughout the country that provide services to dancers, often on a sliding scale.

Organizations have also made inroads in the dance community, supplying periodicals and educational seminars to health care professionals, teachers, and dancers. In the forefront of this movement are the International Association for Dance Medicine and Science, the Performing Arts Medicine Association, Dancers Over 40, the Dance Professionals Associates, and the International Association for the Transition of Professional Dancers. (See the Resource Directory in the back of this book for more information.)

My intention in this book is to restore the joy of dancing by confronting and offering solutions to issues now out of the closet. In the following chapters, you'll learn about dancers' problems from my experience, psychological work, years of advice columns, and surveys of thousands of students, professionals, and retired dancers. For the authors of the countless letters I receive from *Dance Magazine* readers asking for help on many different topics—so many that it's impossible to answer each letter personally—this book is my way of addressing all of your concerns.

In Chapter One, we'll begin with the factors that help to create the dancer in you. If moving to music seems as natural to you as breathing—then you're probably someone who scores high on *kinesthetic intelligence*. Dance training takes you one step further by transforming your body into a finely tuned instrument over a long period. The final outcome will depend, to a great extent, on age, anatomy, parental support, and access to a high level of instruction. To achieve your physical potential, it's important to select the dance technique that's just right for you.

As you'll see in Chapter Two, teaching practices can also have a profound effect on your dancing. Serious dance training is based on the military, where teachers—for better or for worse—exercise considerable authority. One out of every two dancers say they've been unjustly criticized or humiliated in class, and 24 percent have had a teacher who expected them to work with a serious physical problem. Teachers and directors can seem like parents; however, you don't have to accept everything they do on face value. Find out which teaching practices you can trust and why.

In Chapter Three, we'll focus on the influence of body shape and appearance on dancers' self-esteem. All young people face a major transition when they reach adolescence and their bodies begin to change. Sadly, this milestone is often associated with a negative body image in dancers who face an unforgiving mirror and seldom have an ideal thin body. Misinformation about dieting, coupled with a desire to excel at any cost, are a dangerous mix in the dance world, where eating disorders, menstrual problems, and stress fractures are all higher than average. Wouldn't you like to learn how to reach your optimal weight without compromising your energy, health, or career?

In Chapter Four, we'll explore your relationships. To excel, dancers can spend up to sixteen hours a week in class at the advanced level, with little time for socializing outside of work. Competition among dance students, as well as teasing and jealousy from nondancers, can make friendships difficult to sustain. We have found that sexual harassment is also a problem for 16 percent of dancers; young men are the most common targets of this form of abuse. Although there are no easy answers, I will suggest certain strategies that can help you handle your relationships both inside and outside the dance studio.

In Chapter Five, you'll discover how dancers deal with their professional aspirations. Nine out of every ten say it is "very" (58 percent) or "somewhat" (30 percent) important for them to dance on stage. Although dancers pursue this goal with vigor, jobs are hard to find. Only 23 percent of professionals in this country have full-time employment. To be prepared, you need to find a good survival job that will cover your living expenses without wearing you out. Your audition materials should also be in tip-top shape if you want to make a good first impression. Last but not least, all dancers need to use a variety of resources to get work, roles, and promotions.

As you'll discover in Chapter Six, dancers are expected to perform technical feats in front of an audience, even when frightened. Like other athletes, some dancers handle this pressure better than others. Emotional problems that impair performance range from shyness and perfectionism to stage fright. Lack of experience in workshops or onstage can also hurt your dancing. Learn the strategies that Olympic athletes use to achieve peak performance and manage the relationship between mind and body.

In Chapter Seven, we'll take a closer look at dancers' health. As a group, dancers have been found to be healthier than the general population because they are more active, thinner, and less likely to smoke or use illicit drugs. Yet injuries that can curtail serious training or a promising career are a fact of life in dance. Fifty-six percent of leading dancers and 82 percent of elite dance students have been injured. AIDS and eating disorders are also higher than average among dancers. We'll confront these health problems, and discuss current efforts to make health insurance available to all dancers at a reasonable cost.

In Chapter Eight, we'll look at dancers in transition, transitions from dropping out to retiring from a dance career during the mid-thirties because of a loss of stamina due to age. Three out of four dancers will continue to take class, since letting go of the "dancer" identity is like losing your best friend. Mourning this loss takes time. Preparation is also important, beginning at the student level. Meanwhile, new transition centers in the last decade offer career counseling, scholarships, and seminars to help students and professionals bridge the gap to the next phase of their lives.

Dancing is a wonderful vocation—if you know how to handle the inevitable pitfalls along the way. Over the years, I have seen some dancers, with nowhere to turn, become overwhelmed by their problems. Today, I know from personal experience that it's possible to confront the sorrows while embracing the wonders of dance, regardless of your age, stage, or development. Unlike dancers of the past, you don't have to travel this road alone. Be true to your passion—and bring back the joy in dancing!

The idea for this book came from thousands of letters that I've received over the last six years to my advice column in *Dance Magazine*. Many thanks to Editor-in-Chief Richard Philp for his enthusiastic reception of my proposal for the column and his constant support ever since. I'd also like to extend my deepest appreciation to all the dancers who've written to me; your candor and desire to solve problems are truly amazing. Finally, my editor at Jossey-Bass, Alan Rinzler, has made writing this book fun. His comments were positive, sensitive, and constructive—a winning combination!

I would also like to express my thanks to the following people for sharing their expertise in dance as editors, teachers, administrators, doctors, and performers: Ian Betts, Bev & Claudio, Virginia Brooks, Darius Crenshaw, Jacques d'Amboise, Eleanor D'Antuono, Alexander Dubé, Pierre Dulaine, Allison Elner, Robert Fitzgerald, Judith Fugate, Harris Green, William Hamilton, M.D. (orthopedics), Sherrie Hinkle, Katy Keller, P.T. (physical therapy), Pamela Koch (nutrition), Kwikstep & Rocafella, Luigi, Susan Macaluso, Marika Molnar, P.T. (physical therapy), John Olichney, M.D. (hematology), Gary Parks, Germaine Salsberg, Caitlin Sims, Benjamin Soencksen, Ellen Tittler, Michelle Warren, M.D. (endocrinology), and Garielle Whittle.

Last but not least, I'd like to thank my brother, Peter, for his support and friendship, and my parents, Helen and Peter Homek, for introducing me to dance as a child. Their own foray into the arts was inspiring.

# 1

# *A*ccepting the Dancer You Are

*F*alling in love with dancing is magical. It feels predestined, as if you were meant to be a dancer first—and then a human being. But why? Is it your temperament, your character, your physiology? I get letters all the time from frustrated dance students who don't know what it takes to "become" a dancer.

In this chapter we will explore how to make intelligent choices in deciding to dance—by understanding the factors that help to create the dancer in you, by making sure your expectations are realistic for the long run, and by choosing the most appropriate dance technique for who you are.

## What Makes a Dancer

Many factors are important in dancing, from developing sufficient turnout, strength, and flexibility, to simply executing the steps. If you want to progress, you need to set specific goals and then find the best way to achieve them. But first, it's important to know where you stand on the following:

- A sense of "calling" (your passion for dance)

- Kinesthetic intelligence (athleticism, grace, talent)

- Dance training (age when you start; number of classes per week; technique)

- Teachers (competent dance instructors)

- Personality and temperament (drive, resiliency, risk-taking, optimism)

- The right anatomy (genetic destiny)

As you can see, there's a lot more to dancing than just willpower. So let's take a closer look at the various ingredients that help to create the dancer in you.

## A Sense of Calling

Your passion for dance is important, because it helps you to look beyond the immediate blister or missed social event to a higher cause—becoming a dancer. In many ways, a calling keeps you on track. While your friends are hanging out at the mall, you are on a mission to transform your body into a finely tuned instrument. Dancers who are wishy-washy about their work rarely succeed, even if they're talented. In fact, many gifted children get distracted by social interests in adolescence. What then makes a true believer?

The answer can often be found in early childhood. Many dancers report a "crystallizing" experience before the age of five, leading to a deep commitment to dance. Some of these dancers grew up in families where the arts were a large part of their lives, whereas others had parents who were amateur or professional artists themselves. At some point, these children had the good fortune to see a dance performance, hear beautiful music, and *voilà!* They knew that dancing was it.

This was certainly the case for me. My mother was a violinist and my father painted portraits, so I was surrounded by the arts from infancy. According to family lore, I announced my decision to be a dancer after seeing the Royal Ballet perform *Sleeping Beauty* on television at the age of two! By age four I was dancing regularly before a mirror at home and giving impromptu performances at City Center during each intermission of the ballet.

Early exposure to the arts can make a big impression on children in the formative years, laying the groundwork for serious training. Still, it's possible for people to fall in love with dance at any age— through a friend who takes ballet, a touring dance troupe, an old Fred Astaire movie, or simply through serendipity. Students may also develop a passion for dance after the fact. I've known dancers who quit taking class only to discover that something important was missing; other dancers were inspired when a special dance teacher came into their lives. However it happens, a sense of calling is key to your future success, because it gives you a powerful motivation to dance.

### Kinesthetic Intelligence

What makes dancing feel as natural to do as breathing? According to Dr. Howard Gardner, the author of *Multiple Intelligences*, the answer lies in your innate ability to express yourself through movement. This ability, which varies from person to person, occurs along with seven other forms of intelligence: linguistic, logical, musical, naturalist, spatial, and two personal intelligences that help you to understand the motives of others and to know yourself.

Kinesthetic intelligence allows you to move gracefully, while demonstrating your athletic prowess with variations in speed, force, intensity, and direction. If your capacity is deficient in this area, if you are awkward, clumsy, or lack rhythm, dancing is an uphill battle. A thirty-three-year-old unemployed dancer told me that she often cried in frustration because she lacked talent. Although all dancers can improve with hard work and extensive training, your raw physical potential will determine how far you can go in dance. So pay attention to your natural strengths. If these are outside of the kinesthetic realm but you have a knack for logical thinking, dance research may be-up your alley. Verbal skills, on the other hand, could make you a savvy dance journalist.

**Dance Training**

As we've discussed so far, you need to be deeply committed to dance with a natural talent for movement in order to excel. The next step in becoming a dancer is to train your body through repetition and practice. One sixteen-year-old girl told me that she had no idea about how much dance training to get or at what age to get it. This is a common dilemma for dance students, because each technique has different requirements.

If you want to be a professional ballet dancer, it helps to start classes between the ages of eight and ten, when your body is unusually limber. Eight more years of intensive instruction will maintain your natural flexibility, increase the capsular stretch in your hips for turnout (rotation of the legs), and create subtle changes in your anatomy, such as carving out notches in front of the ankle to increase the depth of your plié (knee bends in the turned-out position on one or both legs).

There is no way to hurry up these changes or force your body to adapt. Consequently, dancers who begin ballet training after the age of twelve often have limitations, a fact that can be emotionally devastating to dedicated students. The only exceptions to this rule are adolescent male dancers, students with a background in gymnastics, and the rare "natural" dancer. In the case of men, there is still a negative stereotype in this country that equates dancing with being feminine. Our surveys show that significantly more parents encourage girls to take dance classes compared to boys, with the result that more men wait until after they are even beyond adolescence and in their twenties (which is then too old for ballet) to become dancers. At this point, anatomy becomes the biggest obstacle to a dance career.

If you have had to fight your parents to take dance class, the chances are that you also have moments when you are plagued by insecurity. Dr. Julie Jaffee Nagel has shown that music students who pursue a career in the arts against their parents' wishes get less support over time, thus leading to self-doubt. I discuss how you can turn this around and gain confidence in Chapter Six. For now, be aware that if you've had a late start, it's best to use ballet as a foundation while focusing on other techniques like modern dance, tap, or jazz that take about four years to get the technique down. Ideally, all dance classes should increase from a minimum of two per week to eleven or more at the advanced level.

## Good Teaching

Another piece of the training puzzle depends on your teacher, because dancers learn by watching others first, then putting what they see into practice. The best dance teachers understand the relationship between basic kinesiology and injury prevention, the special needs of children versus adults, and the importance of inspiring dancers to reach their potential by building their self-esteem rather than tearing it down. They should also model exemplary technique, since training is based on imitation.

How do you find a qualified teacher? The easiest way to find a good dance instructor is by attending a well-known academy, an arts magnet (a specialized school that draws from a larger geographical area than the usual school district), or a university-affiliated dance program (see the Resource Directory). The next best choice is to find someone who has trained at one of these institutions and, ideally, has experience as a performer.

Word of mouth can also be a good source for finding a qualified teacher, although it pays to audit a dance class first to make sure that the classroom is safe from abusive teaching practices. I know one emotionally damaged eighteen-year-old girl who refused to audition for a major ballet company after being repeatedly humiliated by her dance teacher, a famous ballerina (see Chapter Two for more on this topic).

Dancers from Alaska to New York have also told me of their difficulties in finding good teachers because of the lack of finances or of dance schools in their area. If you are having a difficult time with these issues, check out the Resource Directory of this book for important information on arts magnet schools, scholarships, and summer programs.

## Personality and Temperament

Just as certain body types are more suited to dance, so may be certain personal qualities. For example, strongly motivated dance students have a big advantage over their peers, because they are able to train even in the face of distractions. Typically, dancers between the ages of fifteen and sixteen are more achievement-oriented than nondancers of the same age. Add to this recipe an optimistic nature, and you will become resilient; you will bounce back from misfortune (like an injury) rather than fall into a quagmire of depression.

In contrast, dancers who are perfectionists often put excessive pressures on themselves. They think, "If I make a mistake on this step, I'm a failure." Yet the fact is that no one is perfect, so demanding a flawless performance is not only impractical but it contributes to low self-esteem. Likewise, a pessimistic attitude will limit your ability to cope with the day-to-day stresses of dance, because your expectations for success are too low.

In my private practice, I often work with dancers who have become their own worst enemies. A sort of self-sabotage affects 16 percent of dancers nationwide. Many underachieve because they have developed a fear of failure or feel unable to live up to a previous success. I know of one fifteen-year-old dancer who refused to return to the School of American Ballet after being promoted, because of her fear that it was only a matter of time before they asked her to leave.

While no dancer likes to fail, real progress comes from seeking out new challenges and learning from past mistakes. In fact, any worthwhile pursuit is usually a struggle until you get it right. Dancers who are afraid to explore and take risks on the road to progress are less likely to achieve long-term success. The good news is that everyone can learn effective coping skills that enhance performance. In Chapter Six, we discuss how to handle competition, promote personal growth, and increase self-esteem so you can perform at your peak.

## Basic Anatomy

Your natural anatomy is the most important factor in becoming a dancer, but also the one that is least likely to be under your control. I've known far too many ballet dancers who were heartbroken because they lacked turnout or their weight didn't conform to the ballet "look." Though it is possible to improve these problems up to a point, you can't change your body completely. Jazz, tap, hip-hop, modern dance, ballroom, and various ethnic dances have different requirements.

How do you decide where your body fits in for dance? One twenty-two-year-old dancer with knock-knees told me that she took four ballet classes a day to improve her turnout until she had a serious knee injury that ended her career. If you are always injured, it's time to visit a dance medicine specialist and find out why. Sometimes, the problem is weakness or a muscular imbalance, in which case you could benefit from a regular exercise program, such as the Pilates method (see the Resource Directory). Anatomy, on the other hand, is destiny, so get feedback from an orthopedist who understands dance.

I often get letters from dancers asking for advice about changing their turnout, flexibility, arches, and muscle mass. I offer suggestions in Chapter Seven, which covers injury prevention. Meanwhile, you can do wonders for your body image and self-esteem if you stop comparing yourself to the ideal ballet body. As you'll see in the following research, very few dancers conform to this image of perfection.

## What the Research Shows

We have found that anatomical problems catch up with many ballet dancers by the advanced level of training. At the School of American Ballet, which is the leading dance academy in the country, we followed a group of adolescent students in the intermediate divisions to see who dropped out of the profession over a four-year period. All of these students had passed a stringent audition to enter the school and were subject to yearly evaluations.

In the first year, 20 percent of the students quit ballet. Dropouts had a number of problems compared to dancers who continued their training:

- An earlier age of menarche (younger than fourteen years old), which is related to larger breasts and hips

- More major injuries, such as torn knee ligaments

- Noticeable muscular weakness

- Reduced flexibility

- Straight legs instead of the slightly bowed legs that make it easier to close in fifth position (feet crossed over heel-to-toe)

- An intense preoccupation with the esthetic standards of ballet that for them were unobtainable

Problems continued to distinguish dropouts during the second year of our study, when 20 percent quit ballet, 22 percent got into a professional ballet company, and 37 percent continued training. The dropouts showed more eating, anatomical, and technical difficulties than the other dancers. These included the following:

- Greater efforts to restrict food intake, leading to deviant eating behavior

- A poorer *pointe* position

- Asymmetrical *relevé* when rising up on *demi-pointe* on the ball of the foot

- Impaired turnout in fifth position

- Muscular tightness in the quadriceps (thighs)

- More knee injuries

- An inability to pirouette to the right side (this skill is associated with eye dominance)

In the final period of our study, 15 percent of the students dropped out of ballet, whereas 22 percent joined a professional company. Our results showed that dropouts had a higher incidence of

- Spondylolithesis (slippage of the vertebra following a stress fracture)

- A poorer height in the *relevé* position

- Impaired turnout in the hips

- Ankle tendinitis

- An anorexic weight (16 percent below ideal weight for height)

- A negative body image

Although none of the problems listed in this study preclude a career in ballet, the competition does make it difficult for dancers without the best bodies to survive at the top. Remember, certain anatomical problems, such as poor turnout and flexibility, are only partially under your control.

## Face the Facts

Fortunately, you can still realize your potential in dance—if you're realistic about your expectations. Take the time to list your own pros and cons in dance. You can then use this knowledge to assess the reality of your expectations when reading this section. Let's look at some examples of dancers who get into trouble.

### The Case of Late Training

| Pros | Cons |
| --- | --- |
| 1. You love dance and commit time and energy to class. | 1. You start serious ballet training five years late. |
| 2. You're a talented dancer and display a high level of kinesthetic intelligence. | 2. Your turnout is poor and you've lost flexibility since childhood. |
| 3. Your personality is well-suited to dancing, due to your discipline and ability to take calculated risks. | 3. Your health is in jeopardy and you need to back off from dance class until you heal. |

This scenario occurs in dancers who are talented, dedicated, and eager to become professionals, yet lack that magic ingredient—early training. If they are unable to cope with this reality, they could become seriously injured and most certainly will face disappointment. A dramatic example is a nineteen-year-old male dancer who became ill and wrote to me asking for advice. Here's what he had to say:

> Three weeks ago I was diagnosed with Hodgkin's lymphoma. The doctor says I have a 75 percent chance of making a full recovery after surgery and chemotherapy. The problem is that I now have to cut back on my dance classes when I really need to catch up. You see, I started ballet last year at age eighteen. And I want nothing less than a few years in a

*major company. Do you think people can be truly happy if they don't realize their greatest dream?*

Right now, this dancer is setting himself up for a big fall, because his late start in dance makes it almost impossible for him to perform ballet professionally in today's competitive job market. Fortunately, this young man has a very good chance of regaining his health and returning to dance class in the future. The more he can adapt to his situation by focusing on what he does have going for him, the better his chances of being happy.

It would also help if this dancer had emotional support during the recovery process instead of toughing it out on his own. Whether you are injured or coming back from a serious illness, this can be a lonely and confusing time for a dancer. The Resource Directory at the back of this book lists health care clinics for performers, many of which offer a variety of services, including psychotherapy, on a sliding scale.

I see other problems with unrealistic expectations in older dancers who tell me that they only take class for fun but then insist on peak performance in spite of their physical limitations. These dancers fail to appreciate their strengths, while focusing on deficits that are beyond their control. In many instances, they feel like failures. Here's a typical example.

**The Case of the Driven Amateur**

| Pros | Cons |
| --- | --- |
| 1. You train in several techniques, giving you more chances to excel. | 1. You begin dance as an adult, so your ability to improve is limited. |
| 2. You have a good teacher who stresses kinesiology. | 2. You have trouble picking up dance routines. |
| 3. You love to express yourself through movement. | 3. You are overly critical of your limitations. |

Many dancers expect more from themselves than they can deliver, making them unhappy even when they are doing well. This was a problem for this dancer, who wrote me with many of the same pros and cons.

> I simply have no talent! After seven years of tap, ballet, and jazz, it takes forever until I can pick up a routine. I'm thirty-six years old. Honestly, should I try to keep on going or hang up my shoes for good?

The decision to dance is very personal and no one can make it but you. I do think, however, that part of this dancer's frustration comes from having goals that are constantly out of reach. Like many dancers, she's fallen into a common trap: failing to live up to her own expectations. If this continues for too long, it can be murder on her self-esteem. To boost her morale—as well as her performance—her goals must be grounded in reality. Let's take a closer look at her situation.

Presently, she's labeling herself "slow" because she believes that she *should* be able to do better after seven years. Is this realistic? After all, she started dance classes when she was twenty-nine years old. Given her late start, she's bound to have some problems. Yet she says that she's able to do the steps, it just takes time. My advice for this dancer is to give herself some credit! If she didn't have talent, she couldn't have come this far. Would it be so terrible if she allowed herself to have fun?

Another classic example of unrealistic expectations is the young dancer who wants to go on *pointe* no matter what! At the School of American Ballet, dancing on toe occurs near the end of the fourth year of training—after you have sufficient strength and technique on *demi-pointe*. Our surveys indicate that hip problems and tendinitis are more common in dancers who go on *pointe* before the age of twelve. Unfortunately, aspiring dance students rarely consider the benefits of waiting a few more years.

## The Case of Toe-Shoe Fever

| Pros | Cons |
| --- | --- |
| 1. You start ballet at the age of eleven, so your body still has time to adapt to the technique. | 1. You can't dance on toe with your friends at age twelve because you need to catch up first. |
| 2. You have a lot of self-discipline and believe in the value of hard work. | 2. Your *pointe* position is poor, due to weakness and lack of technique. |
| 3. Your dance teacher is qualified and supportive. | 3. You compare yourself to your peers and feel bad. |

Being unable to dance on toe often throws dancers into a panic, because it represents an important rite of passage in ballet. The following dancer is obviously at a loss.

> *Help! I'm thirteen years old and still not dancing on pointe. My teacher says I have to wait because I only started ballet two years ago. But it's so hard. Many of the younger girls who started at age eight have toe shoes. Do you think I have any chance of getting them before I die?*

I remember how excited I was to get my first toe shoes, so I can understand this dancer's frustration. A couple of years feels like a lifetime when you're young, yet you've only just begun to acquire the strength and balance necessary for *pointe* work. An easy test to see whether you're ready, used by Dr. Karim Khan, the medical consultant to the Australian Ballet School, is to do *passé*, rising on *demi-pointe* in the turned out position on one leg with the other leg drawn up until the toes touch the front of the knee. Then, let go of any support. If you lose your placement or your standing foot sickles (your weight shifts from the midline to the outer side of your foot), it's too soon to trade in your ballet slippers for toe shoes.

### Set Realistic Goals

If you want to improve in dance, you need to identify your strengths and weaknesses, which means being painfully honest. The next step is to set challenging but realistic goals that are attainable. It sounds easy enough. So why is it so difficult?

When I suggest to frustrated dancers that they take another look at their expectations for success, many panic because of their beliefs about how a "good" dancer should think. Here are some examples:

- Changing my focus means I failed.

- Willpower is always the answer.

- I'll be lost if I don't reach my goal.

- If I change, I'll lose everything.

- I'll never be happy except as a professional dancer.

The dance world teaches us that we can overcome every problem through hard work. This belief makes dancers stand out from the crowd, because many of them are willing to put out maximum energy to achieve their goals. The downside is that it places all of the responsibility on you—even if your body lets you down. Professional athletes who try their best but fail to reach their goals feel less productive. The same goes for dancers whose expectations clash with reality, another reason that it pays to select the best dance technique for you.

## Choose the Right Dance Technique

Once you're ready to put what you know about becoming a dancer into practice, it's time to check out the technique that's just right for you. Are you a high achiever? If so, try to focus on your strengths, particularly if you want to have a career in dance. There are almost twenty thousand professional dancers in the United States—yet 77 percent don't have full-time jobs! On the other hand, dancers who take class simply for pleasure can stick with any technique, as long as they work within the natural limitations of their bodies.

Our research shows that dance students experiment with a wide range of techniques. The most popular forms include ballet (97 percent), jazz (73 percent), modern dance (60 percent), and ballroom (8 percent). Most dancers begin training during childhood; only 6 percent start class when they are seventeen years old or older. Nine out of ten dancers also want to be professionals, yet an appalling 68 percent are unable to achieve the goals that they set for themselves as performers.

## Classical Ballet

Ballet, the most popular but toughest form of dance, is a stylized, rather artificial technique that originated in the courts of Italy and France. Ballet history goes back over three hundred years, and was codified by Carlo Blasis (1797–1878), among others, on whose system classical training is still based. Five positions of the feet form the basis of almost every ballet step, performed with the feet turned out on the floor. There are corresponding positions for the arms, although these vary in number according to the style. Yet you can't learn ballet from a book—you need a teacher to watch over you all the time to prevent injury or even deformity arising from the technique.

As we've already discussed, anatomy is crucial to ballet, because you need turnout and extreme flexibility. Hypermobility, however, is not an asset because it leads to injuries, a subject we cover at greater length in Chapter Seven. Training and genetic destiny create the shape, proportion, and positioning of the body known as "line." To be pleasing, you need to have a special look that comes from long legs, a short torso, nicely arched feet, and a thin body. More than anything, the goal of ballet training is to achieve the greatest control and mobility of your body.

*There are several different styles in ballet. How do you
decide which one is best?*

First, make sure that your teachers are qualified, because good
training is more important than a specific style. The next step is to
see whether any school of ballet suits your body or personality more
than another. For those of you who want to become professionals,
be aware that the only job opportunities, apart from teaching,
choreography, and freelance work, exist in ballet companies, which
sometimes favor a particular style. For example, Boston Ballet uti-
lizes the Vaganova style, whereas Miami City Ballet performs the
Balanchine style.

Let's take a closer look at your choices, beginning with the Cecchetti method, which is good for balance and coordination. Enrico
Cecchetti (1850–1928), an Italian dancer who taught at the Imperial Ballet School in St. Petersburg, developed this style, which
emphasizes line and a clean technique with simple (not flowery)
*port de bras* (arm positions) and ninety-degree extensions (leg lifts).
In contrast, the Soviet teacher Agrippina Vaganova (1879–1951)
devised a lyrical, somewhat more stylized system. The Vaganova
approach stresses big extensions, arched backs, and more *épaule-
ment* (placement of the head and shoulders) at the expense of fast
footwork.

You might also consider training that emphasizes the Britain's
Royal Academy of Dancing (RAD). The syllabus includes both
Cecchetti and Russian elements, offering a wealth of different steps
and combinations. Or, if you're looking for a contemporary version
of the Russian Imperial School, check out the approach created by
George Balanchine (1904–1983). Known for its energy, musicality,
and extremes in movement, the Balanchine style (also referred to
as a technique) is the most accepted American form of ballet. Training focuses on faster, more intricate footwork, greater turnout, and
leg extensions up to your ears. Some dancers stay with one style;
others take the best from each.

Of course, it's easy to get confused when ballet styles use a different name for the same movement. If you need help, check out *The Technical Manual and Dictionary of Classical Ballet* (see Further Reading), which describes each ballet term with a phonetic aid and an illustration. Before long, you'll even know the difference between a Cecchetti and Russian arabesque.

> *My goal is to become a professional dancer. But my body doesn't have the right look for ballet. I'm seventeen years old. What can I do?*

Try not to panic! Your ballet training will help you to be a better dancer in many other techniques that do not rely on a specific body type.

## Modern Dance

Modern dancers, for example, come in all sizes and shapes, and are not as painfully thin as ballet dancers; surveys indicate that modern dancers hover at only 6 percent below their ideal weight for height. According to our research on American, Russian, Chinese, and European dancers, women who become professionals in ballet range between 11 and 15 percent below their ideal weight for height. Male dancers, on the other hand, don't have to worry about their weight, as long as they are at their ideal weight for height and physically fit (see Chapter Three to determine where you are relative to this dimension).

What is modern dance like? In addition to allowing for different body types, modern dance rebels against ballet technique by allowing dancers to experiment in bare feet with new forms of expression and without a language of codified steps. Instead, modern dance has a history of dancers creating their own conventions. Modern dance began around the turn of the last century, and spread quickly in America, which lacked a strong ballet tradition. This dance form then went on to flourish under American female luminaries such as Isadora Duncan and Ruth St. Denis, who proclaimed their emancipation from the confines of the Victorian Age and claimed their right to be seen as individuals.

Current approaches to modern dance are based on the creative talents of Martha Graham, Doris Humphrey, Merce Cunningham, Paul Taylor, and Twyla Tharp, to name a few. Most of the early modern choreographers spawned a unique way of moving based on his or her own theory of its source. This may refer to ethnic traditions, the role of breathing, gravity, or the position of the spine. Modern dance uses the body's weight in deliberate falling, as well as sinuous, angular movements in a multidimensional orientation. Ballet steps, in contrast, are usually performed facing the audience and give the illusion of the dancer's freedom from gravitational pull. Interestingly, there is a growing trend in certain dance companies, such as the Joffrey, to use a hybrid of both techniques, sometimes known as *modern ballet* or *fusion dance*.

An additional benefit of modern dance is that you can perform it in modern dance companies throughout middle age, as opposed to ballet, which weeds out many dancers around the age of thirty. This longevity is evident in the famous Russian ballet dancer Mikhail Baryshnikov, who, at the age of fifty, continues to perform around the world in modern dance. Many modern dancers also teach and choreograph.

## Ballroom Dancing

*I'm in high school and have become increasingly interested in different types of dancing, particularly ballroom. The problem? I need a partner!*

Ballroom is unlike any other form of dance, because you never go solo. Instead, the focus is on how well you and your partner communicate rhythmically with each other. The man, as the leader, initiates changes in movement patterns, while the woman's job is to respond immediately by shifting her weight and direction. This approach differs in the gay and lesbian community, which qualifies partners according to leader and follower and is not gender specific. All dance classes provide people with multiple partners, so you don't need to worry.

Entering a competition is another story. Some ballroom dancers hire their teacher, whom they pay per dance, for pro or amateur competitions held solely in the United States. Other dancers compete in the worldwide amateur divisions by finding a partner at their technical level whose size and leg length is compatible with their own. To find a partner, it's best to advertise by putting up notices in your neighborhood dance studios.

Although it's obvious that ballroom dancing arose years before women's lib, this elegant form of dancing represents a big change in how men and women danced socially together after 1910. Prior to this time, Victorian restraint dominated the scene, and standing a *foot* apart from your partner was standard practice. You were then expected to follow a set sequence of steps—with no room for improvising!

As Victorian society underwent a great social upheaval, new personal freedoms emerged, such as the right of women to vote. Social dancing reflected the *Zeitgeist*, or spirit of the times; dance partners could now make contact with their upper body and arms! Social dancing gained in popularity and dance competitions became an annual event. The international style (formerly known as the "English style") provides a strict definition for five standard dances: the quickstep, slow fox-trot, waltz, Viennese waltz, and tango. Other Latin American dances, which emerged after 1945, became standardized in the mid-1960s. These include the rumba, paso doble, jive, samba, and cha-cha-cha. A recent category that has yet to be included in competitions outside of this country is the hustle, much like the dancing performed by John Travolta in *Saturday Night Fever*.

If you decide to try ballroom, you should know that the smooth, flowing movements come from two kinds of rhythm: body rhythm (your carriage, balance and coordination, leverage and impulse) and step rhythm (the dance pattern to the musical beat). These primary rhythms flow naturally from your body, similar to walking and running, and include walks, boxes, semiruns, and rocks. Your feet should be parallel (no turnout!) while you and your partner move all four legs together in synchronized patterns.

You can practice ballroom for purely social reasons or to enter annual competitions. Classes also help all types of dancers with partnering, according to Pierre Dulaine and Yvonne Marceau, who teach ballroom dancing at Juilliard and the School of American Ballet. There are no specified weight requirements other than cultural, so professional ballroom dancers are usually at or slightly below ideal weight for height. To enter competitions, you'll need a coach to help you prepare your routines and a big allowance—since hotels, air fair, and costumes can make competing pricey, to say the least. Job opportunities include coaching, teaching, choreography, the odd musical, extra work in movies, cabarets, and professional competitions with prize money. By 2008, ballroom dancing may also be part of the Olympics as "dance sport." The first step toward this goal was taken in September 1997 when it was accepted into the Olympic family.

## Hip-Hop

In the mid- to late 1970s, a very different kind of popular dance developed within the hip-hop culture to the accompaniment of heavy electronic music. This dance form, which originated among urban youth, helped to channel their energy away from street gangs into positive interactions. It began with simple footwork patterns, sweeps, and characterizations in park jams (parties in the park) or on linoleum patches laid on a sidewalk.

Over the course of several progressions, five dance styles emerged. *Breakin'* (originally known as *b-boyin'*) involves different footwork and spinning movements on the floor, such as "1990s" where you spin on one hand. Break dancers with a background in gymnastics incorporate back flips and flairs (leg moves originally done on the pommel horse). There are also kung fu moves, owing to the impact of media stars like Bruce Lee and others in the martial arts. A true breaker ends up in a freeze, which is a characteristic pose. The other hip-hop styles focus on upper body movements. With *lockin'*, for example, you use pointing, wrist-rolls, and scoop-hops (jumps). More fluid movements occur in the style of *poppin'*, including waves and hits (robotic contractions to the beat). A more competitive dance form is *uprockin'*, which is similar to the mock battles seen in karate. The most recent hip-hop innovation is the *free style*, which is a fusion of all of the above, as well as jazz and ballet moves like the arabesque (standing on one leg with the other leg raised behind you) and the pirouette.

> *I am a twenty-year-old guy who really wants to do break dancing. Can you tell me how?*

Break dancing can be difficult to do without any prior dance experience. In many ways, it is similar to the floor exercises of gymnastics, which put demands on the neck, arms, shoulders, and back. To get in shape, you should condition your body by doing push-ups for arm, wrist, and shoulder strength; sit-ups for abdominal strength used in backspins and to gain momentum; neck exercises for headspins; and leg exercises for strength in footwork. Though stretching in dance class, aerobic exercises, and gymnastics will help you prevent injuries, please don't try to do head spins without the right supervision!

Job opportunities exist in hip-hop dance companies such as GhettOriginal and Full Circle Productions, hip-hop competitions, and in modern dance companies that use break dancing, such as the Doug Elkin Dance Company. There are no particular weight requirements for men or women. Students should know that Broadway Dance Center is one of the only schools in Manhattan that offers classes on all the hip-hop styles.

## Jazz Dance

Another type of dancing that often appeals to extroverts is contemporary stage dancing, known under the misnomer of "jazz
dancing." What's wrong with the name? Only that jazz music isn't
off-limits to any technique, including ballet! The dance technique
that we think of as jazz has its roots in black social dances of the
nineteenth century and earlier. Around 1910, starting with the
cakewalk and the turkey trot, white social dance adopted diluted
forms of black social dances. Check out jazz dances like the
Charleston, the jitterbug, and twist, and you'll discover movements
that go back to African and early slave dances. Other social jazz
dances, such as the fox-trot, come from European couple-dancing
fitted to jazz rhythms.

Jazz, as a stage dance, comes from these social dances in addition
to the theatrical dance performed in minstrel shows, vaudeville,
early musical comedy, and revues in the nineteenth and early twen-
tieth century. Although theater dance has always been part of the
musical theater, its importance increased with Agnes de Mille's use
of dance to further the plot in *Oklahoma!* (1943). Jerome Robbins
made a remarkable synthesis in his *West Side Story* (1957), along
with Gower Champion in *Hello, Dolly!* (1964) and Michael Bennett in *A Chorus Line* (1976).

The dance style that emerged in the 1950s and 1960s drew as
needed on elements of ballet, tap, and modern dance. Luigi is cred-
ited with creating the first jazz dance technique. Today, jazz dancing
stresses line and a flexible torso, correct footwork performed primarily in the parallel position, and isolated movements that engage multiple body parts, such as the shoulders or pelvis (or, as Luigi says,
"using everything to put it all together"). Dancers trained in modern, tap, and ballet often have trouble isolating their movements,
particularly when several body parts are going in different directions
at once. Jazz dancers also carry their weight close to the floor, unlike
ballet dancers, and often emanate substantial sex appeal.

If you want a professional career doing jazz dancing, it always helps if you can sing and tap dance as well. The weight requirements for women are similar to modern dance. Many jazz dancers find work on cruise ships, industrials, MTV, theme parks, television specials, night clubs, and Broadway shows such as *Cats*.

## Tap Dance

Tap differs dramatically from all other forms of dancing, except flamenco, because it combines sight (something to look at) with sound (the rhythmic tapping of the toe, heels, and flat foot). Tap dancing's first big heyday was in the films and musical comedies of the 1930s and 1940s, although it is a style of American theatrical dance whose roots include the Irish solo step dance, the English clog dance, and African dance movements and rhythms.

The soft shoe, characterized by a smooth, leather-soled style, and the buck-and-wing, a fast style in wooden-soled shoes, preceded taps, which were added in the 1920s when both styles coalesced. Black dancers contributed to new acrobatic styles of tap dance, and jazz musicians provided further rhythmic complexity. The style continued to expand over the next two decades as dancers such as Fred Astaire and Gene Kelly began adding movements from ballet and modern dance. A slew of other talented dancers have made tap what it is today. Savion Glover in *Bring in 'da Noise, Bring in 'da Funk* is taking this art form to a new level.

To get the percussive footwork right in tap, you must combine steps that mark out explicit musical patterns on the floor. This task requires coordination, loose ankles and legs, and lots of rhythm, with your body weight carried low to the ground. The successful result depends on the dancer's skill, which tap is hit, where, and how hard. Dancers who train only in ballet often have trouble shifting to tap, because they find it difficult to let their weight fall into the ground and to relax their legs and feet. Still, if you want to perform in musicals, you'll need some background in ballet, as well as in jazz. It also helps to sing and act.

Other job positions in tap include performing in tap dancing companies and jazz clubs, concert work, and conducting workshops. There's also a big market in Europe and South America for tap dancers who teach and give solo performances. Many professional engagements come from teaching foreign dance instructors who invite you back to their country. Body weight requirements are similar to modern dance and jazz.

*I'm interested in becoming a Rockette. Could you give me information on the requirements?*

The requirements for Rockettes are unique. First, you have to have a height of five feet, five and one-half inches or taller to qualify. And don't bother fibbing, because they measure you in your stocking feet! Then you'll be asked to perform a jazz and tap combination, plus a high kick if you get called back. In addition to being talented, you'll also need to have a nice figure and be thin (although not as thin as a ballet dancer). The final aspect is personality—sort of like Miss America. This will be your moment to shine. So, if they ask you on videotape why you want to be a Rockette, be prepared!

---

As you can see, dance varies dramatically in terms of the mode of performing (singing, dancing in one or more techniques), personality (controlled, sexy, elegant), body type (weight, shape), and codified steps. Ballet is the most exacting because even with enthusiasm, talent, and dedication, you can't work magic without the right body or adequate training. This is why you need to be realistic and make the right choice for you.

Let me tell you a story about a dancer who struggled with this problem of choice. "Julie" had started ballet at the age of sixteen. She knew that she was behind her peers and was determined to do everything in her power to catch up with them in class. By the time I met her six years later, she was taking tap and jazz, singing, and going to a lot of auditions. The problem was that she had little kinesthetic ability, being awkward and slow to pick up combinations.

We got to work and began to look at her options. As it turned out, Julie had a wonderful personality that was bubbly and effervescent. She also loved to express her feelings and was a natural at acting. After much indecision (because she felt like a traitor to dance), Julie settled into a commercial acting class and was delighted to get several television commercials. While she continues to take dance classes and to do the odd musical theater audition, her self-esteem has improved tremendously by focusing on her natural strengths rather than her weaknesses. The last I heard, Julie had become a successful actress, winding up with the leading role in a made-for-TV movie.

By now you realize that becoming a dancer depends on many factors: passion, kinesthetic ability, dance training, competent teachers, personality, and *anatomy*. Remember, only some of these factors are under your control; it's up to you to be realistic by setting reasonable goals and choosing the dance technique that's just right for you. As you'll see in Chapter Two, a large part of your approach to dance will come from teaching practices, which affect your confidence, injury patterns, and professional aspirations. To make the most of your potential, you need to choose dance teachers you can trust.

# Teaching Practices
## *The Good, the Bad, the Ugly*

*D*o you remember your first dance teacher? I have a vivid memory from the age of eight, entering a studio at the old School of American Ballet on West 83rd Street and Broadway. Dressed in a new black leotard, ballet slippers, and bright pink tights, visions of glory danced through my head—until I spied my teacher. Madame Antonina Tumkovsky stood near the piano, giving each of us a curt greeting in a thick Russian accent. Her imperious manner told me in no uncertain terms that there would be no daydreaming about tutus and bouquets in her class. Exactly what had I gotten myself into?

Whether you're young or old, at the professional level or still in training, class is an indispensable part of being a dancer. For that, you need a teacher who—just like a parent—will play a crucial role in your life. In my case, I was fortunate that all of my teachers in the School of American Ballet were highly talented, sensitive instructors. Other dancers aren't so lucky. I've heard for years about abusive teaching practices, and my research confirms that it exists. This chapter shows you the good side of dance training, but also how teaching practices can go wrong, and ways to choose the right school for you.

# The Benefits of Good Dance Training

To appreciate the advantages that dancers gain from taking class, it's important to understand the context. Enrolling in a dance academy is a lot like enlisting in the military. Aside from learning the fine points of a specific technique, your teachers demand obedience—no ifs, ands, or buts about it. Most students catch on quickly, applying themselves diligently to the task at hand. Over time, dance training teaches you discipline, good work habits, and a positive approach to feedback—attributes that transfer readily to areas outside of the profession. Let's take a look at the teaching practices that contribute most to your development.

## Discipline

One of the first lessons you learn in dance training is to make exercise a regular part of your life. Dance teachers expect you to take weekly classes to improve your strength, flexibility, timing, and technique. As a result, discipline is reinforced at every step of the way. You may be stiff, sore, or exhausted, but you'd better be stoic and avoid cutting class without permission. If you do goof off for a couple of weeks, a dance academy may put you on probation or even strip you of your scholarship.

Dance teachers emphasize the importance of discipline through rules: dancers should not talk, chew gum, wear improper attire, or behave in a disorderly way in class. Many also disapprove of their students taking class in other studios, as you'll see in this letter from a concerned mother.

> I'd really like to know why school directors don't want their upper-level students to take instruction (or roles) at other schools. My daughter's school isn't using her for anything special, so what is the logical reason for their fanatic attendance-taking and threats of expulsion for missed classes?

Dance schools are commonly possessive about students. The reasons are partly territorial, but a school may also have its own style of training, based on an influential choreographer (such as Balanchine) or a unique technique (such as Graham's). Many school directors believe that conflicting teaching methods confuse young students and teach them bad habits. Though some schools are more stringent about attendance than others, this is rarely a problem if there's a good fit between you and your dance program.

Dance training teaches you to practice consistently, because the body—like a piano—must be finely tuned. Our surveys show that dancers take an average of six ninety-minute classes per week; however, this number can easily triple for some overachievers. Eight out of ten dancers also make a point of adding other exercise programs to their regime. Besides class, these dancers usually work out three days a week lifting weights or doing an aerobic activity.

What does the rest of the world do? Although most people know that regular exercise leads to better health and weight maintenance, only 15 percent exercise all the time; 30 percent are completely sedentary. In contrast, dancers work out regularly in their teens and twenties; six out of ten also take weekly classes into middle age and beyond!

For example, this is an ordinary week in a dance student's life: "Vanessa" is a sixteen-year-old junior in high school who takes daily ballet classes with a good teacher. Recently, her orthopedist suggested that she add Pilates exercises—a popular workout program that emphasizes strength and flexibility in the turned-out position—to help her recover from a sprained ankle and prevent further injuries. She now works out three extra times a week, doing a series of exercises on her back to increase her strength and flexibility. The last item on Vanessa's agenda includes swimming every other day to control her weight. Dancing isn't aerobic, so it doesn't burn a lot of calories.

Though it's easy to see how Vanessa's discipline works with exercise, this ability is also useful outside of dance. I know dancers who also study acting and singing, go to school, and raise a child without blinking an eye! Once you've mastered the rules and regulations of dance, you can use this discipline the rest of your life.

## Work Habits

Along with acquiring discipline, students also learn constructive work habits in dance, which, as you know, can take up to eight years to master. To attain a specific technique, dance teachers encourage students to put out maximum effort, analyze mistakes, and try again after they fail. Numerous studies agree that dancers, as a group, are more achievement-oriented than their nondancing peers. The fact is that dance training teaches you to overcome obstacles.

I know one twenty-one-year-old male dancer who was unable to lift women because of a weak upper body. Instead of giving up on him in adagio class, his dance teacher analyzed his physical deficits, offered solutions like weight training and technical changes, and encouraged him to persevere. This dancer eventually became a strong adagio partner because of this approach. An unexpected benefit came when he used these same work habits in his required academic courses at the Juilliard School, where he was a dance major, and graduated with straight A's in all of his college classes. Did the teaching practices in dance help this student to excel in his academic courses?

According to Heather Fletcher, a dancer and 1996 semifinalist in the Westinghouse Science Talent Search, the answer is yes. Her research shows that the work habits you pick up from dance training add significantly to your grade-point average in school! My own investigations of dancers confirm these results. In a national survey that I conducted in *Dance Magazine* of almost a thousand readers, three out of five dancers were excellent academic students irrespective of their grade level; only 5 percent were C students, and a mere 1 percent got D's. Dance training teaches you to keep going when times get tough by learning from mistakes. As you'll see, this approach is very special.

Unlike activities that focus primarily on outcome, dance training emphasizes effort. Mr. Balanchine, my former boss at the New
York City Ballet, used to tell us to "run like mad" when he wanted
his dancers to travel across the room. It didn't matter if we landed
on our rumps, so long as we put our heart and soul into trying to
cover the space. He would also have us experiment with different
movements to facilitate our goals, even if this changed the choreography. The moral of the story? Nothing is set in stone. Just keep
trying to do your best, analyze your mistakes, and eventually you'll
see improvement.

Carol Dweck, a Columbia University psychologist, shows us how
important this approach is to success. Her research shows that gifted
children who go on to excel in their area of talent have a unique
outlook: They believe that the harder they try, the better they get.
In contrast, less successful but equally gifted children believe that
they have a fixed amount of talent and ignore the power of elbow
grease. Let's look at how these differences add up.

1. *Successful students*. These children follow an "incremental
   theory," believing that effort—rather than perfection—is the
   biggest factor to their overall success. If they fail at a task,
   they look at it as a problem to solve rather than a reflection of
   their ability. As a result, they tend to seek out new challenges
   and learn from past mistakes.

2. *Unsuccessful students*. Unlike the first group, these students go
   by an "entity theory"; they see themselves as having only a
   fixed amount of their special gift. When they make a mistake,
   they interpret this as a sign that they are less gifted in their
   eyes and in the eyes of others. It's impossible to be perfect, so
   these children often hold back, a trait that makes them less
   likely to succeed.

As you can see, the work habits that you acquire as a student
have a huge impact on your performance. A good dance teacher

helps you to understand that the learning process is rarely smooth. Instead, hard work pays off, as long as you can discover what went wrong and learn from your mistakes.

## The Use of Feedback

Another potential benefit of good teaching practices comes from the use of feedback. A teacher's praise, criticism, and disinterest tell you volumes about your dancing. Years before I understood my Russian ballet teacher's exclamation of *"pahchyeemoo?"* ("why?" is the literal translation), I relied on her tone of voice to tell me that I needed to improve my performance. Later, I learned through my research on the New York City Ballet that although all dancers enjoy being praised, six out of ten dancers also believe that criticism is positive because it provides useful feedback and forces them to work harder to gain a teacher's approval.

Feedback also offers vital clues about what a teacher is "looking for" in you. If you believe in this person's expertise, it becomes doubly important to decipher the message, understand its meaning, and correct the problem.

> *I've heard it said that a good teacher helps dancers to develop not only technical and artistic skills, but a belief in their ability to dance. Is this true?*

Absolutely! Nothing beats a teacher's encouraging tone of voice or thoughtful corrections, as many dance students can attest. Unfortunately, a crowded class often makes getting sufficient feedback about your dancing difficult. This is particularly problematic at the professional level.

I met one twenty-three-year-old professional dancer in my consulting room who'd been feeling lost ever since she joined her dance company. There were so many people in company class that it was difficult to get attention. This young dancer didn't want to just get by, like some of the older company members, by using class to warm up without improving her technique—but what, if anything, could she do?

When I see new company members, I often spend time telling them about the way a dance company works. The reality is that teachers may conduct daily class, oversee rehearsals, replace injured dancers, and work out the next day's schedule—all within a twenty-four-hour period! Needless to say, their minds may be elsewhere when it comes to helping you with the fine points of your dancing. Once our young dancer understood this fact, she found a gifted teacher outside the company who gave her the attention she needed.

If we now take all of this information together, we can see that dance training teaches dancers discipline, excellent work habits, and an ability to use feedback—attributes that are going to be assets everywhere! This fact is being touted on a global scale by organizations interested in "recycling" dancers after they retire in their thirties from performing. The thinking goes: "Few people work as hard as dancers, so let's use this untapped resource in the job market."

On a personal note, my work ethic was of enormous help to me in psychology, from finishing my dissertation to creating my advice column, which reaches more than 230,000 readers. Remember, whether you become a professional dancer or go into another career, your dance training will teach you more than a technique. You'll also learn a positive approach to work that will help you to handle other challenging jobs.

Now that you know the benefits of dance training, it's time to discuss a thornier issue: the pitfalls stemming from a teacher's abuse of power. All dance teachers aren't created equal; some are better equipped at instructing students than others. So let's see how to tell whether your teachers are allies, benevolent gods, or tyrants.

## Negative Teaching Practices

It's common for dance teachers to point out mistakes and encourage dancers to keep working in the face of pain. These practices are useful up to a point: They keep you focused on improvement while training you to ignore minor discomforts that distract you from your goal. Yet some teachers go too far.

In my survey of almost a thousand dancers, I came up with some alarming results. Almost half (48 percent) of this group reported that they'd been unjustly criticized or humiliated by a dance teacher in class. Almost one out of four (24 percent) dancers also said that a teacher had expected them to keep working with a serious injury. Teaching practices like these can hurt your health and well-being. Check out the damage that these dancers suffered.

### Verbal Attacks

Researchers who've studied bullying by teachers say it has three basic components: its intent is negative and hurtful; it's repeated over time; and there's an imbalance of power between the attacker and the victim. Only 2 percent of regular students say this has happened to them compared to 48 percent of dance students. One dancer told me that her teacher often singled her out for no reason, making the other kids laugh at her by saying, "Stupid, fat pig, maybe you should quit—you're hopeless." Bullying from one's classmates can cause persistent self-blame and feelings of worthlessness. What happens when it's your teacher who's the bad guy?

Dance students who've been bullied by their teachers report significantly more symptoms of stage fright. When doing a step, they're less able to concentrate, they may feel a sense of dread, and often tremble or get sick to their stomachs. Yet they rarely give themselves a break. Instead, I found that these dancers are more likely to keep working when injured compared to students without an abusive teacher.

The result can be a disaster! Verbally harassed dancers report more injuries to the foot, knee, back, hip, and ankle than those without harsh teachers. They also rely on more health-care providers, such as orthopedists and therapists for emotional stress, and fail to achieve their goals as professionals because of problems with self-

**Table 2.1. Percentage of Dancers Reporting Problems in Relation to Teacher Bullying.**

| Problem Reported | Dancer Was Bullied | Dancer Was Not Bullied |
|---|---|---|
| *Mental Problems* | | |
| Excessive fear | 16 | 12 |
| Mental anxiety | 18 | 9 |
| Physical anxiety | 14 | 6 |
| Constant alarm | 12 | 7 |
| *Physical Problems* | | |
| Arthritis | 19 | 11 |
| Stress fracture | 21 | 11 |
| Chronic injuries | 59 | 45 |
| Tendinitis | 47 | 31 |
| *Career Problems* | | |
| Self-sabotage | 20 | 9 |

sabotage. Examples of self-sabotage include overwork, engaging in substance abuse, and avoiding auditions. Table 2.1 shows how mental and physical problems increase significantly for dancers who've experienced bullying from their dance teacher in class.

Dancers need to have feedback about their work, which means being open to criticism. Teachers have the power to make this learning experience positive. The best teachers take a problem-solving approach to mistakes rather than making things personal. They also set up specific goals that don't escalate as soon as you reach them. Otherwise, you may push your body until either it or you give up. The numbers in Table 2.1 tell a disturbing story. Here's a letter from a dance student whose teacher caused her a lot of mental anguish.

*I have a real problem—my teacher hates me! We used to be really close, only she kept asking for more. I did what she asked, but it was never enough. Then she started screaming and cursing me out in class. It was so loud, I just wanted to die. I don't see her anymore, but I feel really bad about myself.*

If a public school teacher acted like this, she would be kicked out of the system. Why should you have to put up with it in dance class? Almost every dancer who's come to see me for counseling has had at least one abusive teacher in the past. It's simply not professional—and, as you know, it can also be a real blow to your ego. When bullying occurs, it's important to speak to the director of your school. Classrooms need to be safe for dancers. Your self-esteem, not to mention your career, may depend on it!

## Working When Injured

Similar problems occur when teachers expect dancers to work with a serious injury. Can you imagine pushing yourself with a sprained ankle or a torn knee cartilage? Dancers who work with an injury report full-blown cases of stage fright, as well as significantly more injuries to the shoulder, knee, foot, back, hip, and ankle. As you can see in Table 2.2, these dancers fail to reach their goals as performers as a result of more injuries, self-sabotage, and poor health. They also use more support services like psychotherapy.

I wish I could say that these problems stop after you get to the professional level—but the truth is depressing. I know of some extremely powerful choreographers who regularly treat a serious injury as though it was all in the dancer's head. When these choreographers finish a dance piece for the season, the company's physical therapy room is often teeming with injured dancers, some of whom may stay out of commission for as long as two years. These choreographers only care about their work, not the price in human suffering. To them, a dancer is expendable.

**Table 2.2. Percentage of Dancers Reporting Problems Working with Injuries.**

| Problem Reported | Dancer Was Expected to Dance with a Serious Injury | Dancer Was Not Expected to Dance with a Serious Injury |
|---|---|---|
| *Mental Problems* | | |
| Stage fright | 14 | 7 |
| *Physical Problems* | | |
| Arthritis | 21 | 13 |
| Stress fracture | 27 | 13 |
| Chronic injuries | 66 | 48 |
| Tendinitis | 52 | 34 |
| *Career Problems* | | |
| Injuries | 24 | 14 |
| Self-sabotage | 21 | 13 |
| Poor health | 9 | 2 |

One twenty-two-year-old dancer at a national ballet company told me that she'd been ecstatic to see her name on the day's rehearsal sheet for a new piece. It was scheduled for the gala on opening night in New York! Unfortunately, problems began with the first rehearsal. The choreographer demanded that everyone perform full-out, even though many of the steps were dangerous. This dancer threw herself into the piece before she and her partner were ready. When she fell out of a particularly risky lift and hurt her hip, the choreographer insisted that she continue rehearsing. A week later, after performing in constant pain on tour, she sought out an orthopedist. To her horror, she discovered that a muscle had pulled a small piece of bone loose from her pelvis. Instead of a starring role, this dedicated dancer sat in the audience for the first three weeks of the company's winter season at Lincoln Center.

Dancers are vulnerable. Because they love their work, it's easy to coerce them into dancing with a serious injury. Furthermore, a teacher or choreographer who makes a dancer feel guilty about taking time off sends a message that injuries aren't acceptable! Yet, the fact is that there's a big difference between good pain (associated with progress) and bad pain (which means you're hurting your body).

## Do You Pay?

Throughout the previous section, I discuss teaching practices that may damage your emotions, body, and career. Now it's time to assess the damage that's been done. Let's begin with your mental attitude.

Abusive behavior by someone in authority colors the way you feel about yourself over time. You're the victim, yet it's normal to blame something that you did, because this makes the situation seem less dangerous. Like an abused child, you believe: "If I was *really* good, then I'd be treated better." Here are some examples of what often goes through an abused dancer's mind.

- I did that step horribly. My teacher's right to pick on me.

- How can I expect anyone to like me, when I dance this badly.

- I know I'm stupid, fat, and ugly.

- Why do I always do everything wrong?

I know one twenty-six-year-old dancer who had a highly critical teacher from childhood. Now he finds that he is overly critical of his own performance. By the time Thursday comes around each week, he's ready to quit because, "I can't believe how lazy I am." As it turns out, he's exhausted after rehearsing six hours a day, pushing himself in company class, and performing nightly. This dancer needs to change his attitude, as well as his approach to work.

In my clinical practice, I've found that self-doubt can lead to low self-esteem. You may start to label your dancing as bad or believe that everyone sees you in the same negative light as your teacher. To counteract these thought patterns, try to be fair. In Chapter Six, which deals with peak performance, I show you ways to counteract negative thoughts. Right now, I want you to pay attention to when you criticize yourself. Remember, before you label yourself as lazy or untalented, consider that the problem may derive from a sadistic, critical teacher or from a temporary factor, such as fatigue. If this is so, please give yourself a break! Don't forget, destructive teaching practices put all dancers at significant risk for mental and physical distress. These practices are particularly destructive when they occur under the guise of training you to be stoic and self-critical. Though there are many excellent dance teachers, we need to guard against authority figures who abuse their power while endangering dancers' health and well-being.

## Choosing the Right School

Now that you know what teaching practices to avoid, it's time to assess your situation. Dance classes involve a big investment of your time, energy, and money. In the first chapter, I gave you a quick summary of the factors associated with success in each dance form, including your training. Let's consider what goes into choosing a good dance school.

While geography and finances can limit your choices, the easiest way to ensure quality dance training is to attend a school that has a good reputation or one that's associated with a major dance company (especially if you want to be a professional dancer). The same goes for a specific dance teacher. Scholarships and summer dance programs can help you out if you're broke or stuck in the boondocks, so check out the Resource Directory at the back of the book. Remember, before committing yourself to a dance school, try to audit a couple of classes and talk to dancers enrolled in the program.

Then, ask yourself these questions:

1. Do I fit in with the level of competition in this school?
2. Is the classroom safe from negative teaching practices?
3. Does the school's atmosphere, philosophy, and faculty inspire me as a dancer?

Let's go over each of these areas in terms of your present dance school.

## Level of Competition

If you feel at odds with your dance school, it's possible that you don't fit in with the competition. Many serious dancers feel stifled at second-rate dance schools with inferior teachers. Other dancers get into top-notch schools by the skin of their teeth, but are unable to do more than survive. How do you know if the competition in a dance school is right for you? Let's see how one mother handled this dilemma.

"Jenny" is twelve and wants to be a professional dancer. But she has a long torso and short legs. Her mother researched the dance schools in their neighborhood, finding that the top school was in ballet. It was also highly competitive: She learned that one out of every two children failed the initial audition, and the faculty continued to weed out students without the right bodies. A second ballet school had open classes with no entrance audition, and a third dance academy held auditions and offered classes in ballet, modern dance, and jazz.

Which school did Jenny attend? After discussing the problem with several people in the dance profession, including me, Jenny's mother decided to send her daughter to the third school. Why?

First, Jenny's new dance school offers a variety of dance techniques, giving her more chances to excel with her particular body type. Her mother also likes the idea that many advanced dancers in this school go on to attend a college dance program. She thinks, "If Jenny doesn't get a job as a dancer, at least she'll have a college degree."

In fact, many modern and jazz dancers graduate from college before pursuing a successful career on the stage, in teaching, and in choreography. Occasionally, a ballet dancer will perform after graduation by joining one of the few ballet companies associated with a college dance program. Be aware, however, that most ballet companies choose dancers right out of high school—or even earlier. I was only fifteen when I apprenticed with the New York City Ballet, and they asked me to join the company five months later!

If you're interested in finding a college dance program, a good place to begin your search is the *Dance Magazine College Guide*, which provides facts on programs across the country (see the Resource Directory). Contact the school directly to find out more about the type of dance training (the most common programs offer modern and ballet). Don't forget to make an appointment with your high school guidance counselor, because there's more to choosing a college than just reading books. Friends also can help by sharing their experiences in various programs.

Of course, it's possible that you may still be confused about choosing the right college dance program. Check out this next letter from a concerned student.

> *My goal is to dance with the Martha Graham Dance*
> *Company. But there's a problem: I was trained incorrectly*
> *for the first three years. I'm now applying for college dance*
> *programs and know that schools like Juilliard would never*
> *accept me. Would the Graham company accept dancers*
> *from a less well-known school?*

The short answer is yes. In fact, dancers who set their sights on a specific dance company should be well versed in the specific technique. In terms of the Graham company, you should know that it's somewhat rare for a dancer who hasn't attended the Graham school to be accepted into the Graham company. The Martha Graham School of Contemporary Dance offers a two-year certificate program for high school graduates. This program, which is performance-oriented, includes classes in technique, repertory, composition, and music. Some financial aid is available.

If you want to go to college first, be sure to choose a school that includes Graham technique as part of its dance program. A few examples include Florida State University, Cornish College of the Arts in Seattle, the Meadows School of the Arts at Southern Methodist University in Dallas, and the University of Michigan. Of course, there are many other good colleges; just be sure to ask about the type of dance training.

### Classroom Safety

Once you've dealt with the competition problem, the next step is to evaluate a dance school's teaching practices. A no-pain, no-gain attitude dominates dance training. In the past, some teachers would actually brandish canes, yell, and verbally attack students in an unexpectedly fierce manner—all in the service of making them into better dancers. Although this approach is rare in the best dance schools, you've seen that, in the absence of national teaching standards, it still exists throughout the country for 48 percent of dancers. As a result, it's up to students to judge whether a classroom is safe from verbal and physical abuse, or else suffer the consequences. Check out the following warning signs.

1. *Impatience*. Does your teacher boil over at the drop of a hat? If so, watch out! This teacher may overreact to ordinary mistakes, making the classroom a dangerous place. Remember, students who succeed aren't afraid to fail, so long as they learn from their mistakes. Find a teacher who makes it safe to struggle with a dance step, because this is how to learn real mastery. I know one eighteen-year-old dancer who became much less fearful of taking risks after working with a new teacher who didn't pounce on her.

2. *Focusing on the negative*. All dancers need feedback to help them improve their dancing. Unfortunately, some teachers only

focus on problems, while ignoring signs of progress. The result is that dancers often feel worthless. This is what happened to a twenty-four-year-old modern dancer until he found a teacher who also paid attention to what he was doing right. A teacher's feedback affects your self-worth. Rather than developing low self-esteem or worse—depression—pick a dance teacher who gives you credit when credit is due.

3. *Making inappropriate comparisons.* Teachers often use talented dancers as role models for other students, asking them to demonstrate a step or drawing your attention to some aspect of their technique. This teaching practice is useful up to a point; it is destructive when it is used as a way to humiliate others. For example, a teacher who says, "Look at how well Mary spotted during her double pirouette," is showing you how it looks to do the step correctly. On the other hand, if your teacher's habit is to sneer, "You can't do steps Mary can do in her sleep," it's time to find another teacher.

4. *Ignoring injuries.* The biggest problem to look out for is a negative approach to injuries. Does your teacher, for example, call a student lazy if she asks to cut out jumps because her doctor says that the only way her chronic tendinitis will heal is to not do jumps? Some dance teachers act like an injury is simply an excuse to goof-off. In one study of students in Ontario, 43 percent kept dancing against their doctor's advice. They also said that their injuries were not taken seriously by their teachers. Your dance teacher should know what your doctor recommends, then follow it.

Altogether, a safe approach to dance training can help you to

- Reach out and meet new challenges

- Cope with disappointments

- Establish healthy work habits

- Feel like you're able to achieve results

Don't settle for anything less!

### Does Your Teacher Inspire You?

Now that you know how to recognize negative teaching practices, it's time to move on to a loftier goal—inspiration! The fact is, dance training can get boring. Day after day, year after year, for as long as you want to dance, you must repeat the same steps to achieve a high level of mastery, maintain your technique, and stay in shape. Even if you're madly in love with dancing, a dull routine can easily become monotonous.

Fortunately, talented teachers know how to make dance training an exciting event. Instead of giving the same old *barre* every day in class, they make a point of adding a variety of steps, explaining the purpose of the exercise, or tying movements together with interesting choreography. They also know how to help students improve their dancing without overwhelming them with constant corrections.

Multiple corrections make it difficult for a dancer to focus on a problem long enough to solve it. They also create considerable psychological stress for the dancer who feels justifiably that nothing that is performed is any good. One young ballerina would come to me after a rehearsal feeling beaten down by her director's unending corrections, which would change arbitrarily on a daily basis. To all the world, it looked as though this director had no idea what he was after. And neither did the dancer!

I know another talented jazz student who came to New York but doubted her ability to compete. She wondered, "Am I really good enough to get a role in a Broadway show?" To help her out, we located a wonderful teacher who inspired her to be her best, technically and artistically. In each class, this dance teacher set up specific, well-defined goals to help correct her weaknesses while capitalizing on her strengths. Her teacher's feedback was also geared toward a problem-solving approach, emphasizing effort rather than perfection. Finally, she never gave more than a few corrections, such as adjusting her placement, in each class. By the time this dancer auditioned for *The King and I*, she was confident and strong, and got the part.

A teacher's inspiration can do wonders for your performance. In sports, Coach Effectiveness Training (CET) workshops are capitalizing on this knowledge by offering guidelines for communicating effectively with young athletes, earning their respect, and getting along with their parents. The results are encouraging, according to research on five outcome variables, including coaching behavior, children's self-esteem, attitudes, stage fright, and dropping out of training. Make sure you find a dance teacher whose inspiration brings out the best in you.

---

The point of this chapter is to highlight the many benefits of dance training, as well as describe how teaching practices can go wrong. Another factor we should keep in mind is prevention. The Healthier Dancer Programme in the United Kingdom recommends that the teaching process should include specific knowledge of how the body functions, ranging from optimal nutrition to the importance of cooling down after class to reduce muscle soreness and stiffness. I believe we need to take this one step further by establishing national teaching standards in this country, with required courses in kinesiology, injury prevention, and child psychology. Dancers also need to be educated about how to cope with occupational stress.

In the next chapter, I discuss another pressure that teachers often place on dancers—weight loss. Although there are many obstacles to achieving an ideal body in dance, it is possible to achieve an optimal weight without compromising your health!

# $\mathscr{F}$ocusing on Body Shape and Appearance

*I*n a just world, dancers would be judged on their musicality, talent, and physical grace. Yet the first thing the audience spots is—the body. That's why even ballerinas worry about their weight and students who are desperate to change their appearance ask me for advice. Many of these dancers have already pushed themselves to the limit with starvation, compulsive exercise, or unsuccessful trips to the plastic surgeon. They're at a loss as to what to do next.

This chapter tells you how to reach your optimal weight without compromising your health or career. First, I discuss why your body looks the way it does and show you the formula for finding your ideal weight on a chart. Then, we review the behaviors that often get dancers into trouble, such as crash diets and serious eating disorders. In the last section, you'll discover the benefits of a sensible approach to weight loss that really works!

## About You and Your Body

Many young dancers want me to predict their future. They send pictures of themselves from dance class, they tell me their height and weight, and they ask the same question: "Can I be a professional with my body?" Unfortunately, it's difficult, perhaps impossible, to look at a young student and tell who will make it into a dance company. It's also true that a dancer with a less than perfect body but with enough talent may become a pro. Still, your training and genetic makeup will affect your physical development. Here is why.

### The Effects of Dance Training

Weekly dance classes change your body over a period of years. For example, the repetitive movements of a *grand plié* slowly mold notches in the front of your ankles, while the bones are growing. Stretching your muscles and tendons improves flexibility and turn-out, whereas jumping increases the density in your bones.

Along with these changes, dance training also affects your body shape and size by determining how fast you mature. Research shows that girls who take dance class often have a delay in menarche past the average age (approximately twelve) as a result of physical exercise, particularly if they start their training during *early* childhood. Though there are exceptions to every rule, this delay is associated with a longer, leaner, more linear body. Boys who exhibit a delay in beard growth and voice change are also significantly thinner than those who mature earlier.

On average, female dancers begin to menstruate around the age of fourteen, with most breast development occurring two years later. While this is good for dancing, it may be difficult to fit in with the kids in high school. This happened to one tearful ballet dancer, who told me that she was the only one among her peers without a training bra. The boys called her "Surfboard" because of her flat chest, making her feel highly self-conscious. The good news is that once you grow up, most people admire you for being physically fit. In fact, dancers have a reputation for having great bodies!

### Weight and Your Genes

Genetic endowment also affects how your body looks. If your parents are chubby, the chances are that you will be, too. Studies show that family resemblances in weight can run as high as 70 percent. This relation occurs across the whole range of body fatness, from very thin to very fat. This doesn't mean that diet and exercise are unimportant in determining weight—in fact, they can be extremely effective with the right approach. Clearly, however, genes play a significant role in your eventual body shape and size.

Let's see how this process works. "Ginny," a beautiful dancer from New Jersey, comes from a family of plump women. Her best friend "Lara," who lives next door, has thin parents. Both girls take dance class together and like to indulge occasionally in junk food, such as hot dogs, fries, and burgers. Yet Lara remains thin, while Ginny notices that she gains weight easily.

Is this unfair? You bet it is! Unfortunately, I know a number of heavy dancers who never eat junk food. In fact, my research on professional ballet dancers shows that heavier dancers eat 900 fewer calories per day than thinner dancers. Yet I continue to hear stories about dance teachers who tell their students to go on banana and yogurt diets or just go hungry. Instead of advising heavy dancers to go on crash diets (which are dangerous and rarely produce results), it's better to refer them to a nutritionist or weight loss specialist who can review their history and make suggestions based on their unique needs.

## Can Dancing Make You Thin?

So far, I've discussed how dance training, its effect on pubertal development, and your ancestors all play a role in the way you look. But what about dancing to lose weight?

Although exercise is a great way to get rid of excess pounds, dancing rarely helps you out. I know one nineteen-year-old dancer who was determined to lose weight: She took four dance classes a day and rehearsed in workshops in her spare time. At the end of each day, she was exhausted. Yet she couldn't make her weight conform to the standards of the school director. What this dancer didn't know was that dancing isn't aerobic: the most taxing variation only lasts about four minutes, so even a one-hour ballet class burns only 200 to 300 calories. Other dance forms, which are less physically demanding than ballet, also do little toward weight loss.

### How Thin Should You Be?

In my surveys of professional dancers from America, China, Russia and Western Europe, women's weights in ballet range from 10 percent to 15 percent *below* their ideal weight for height. Just in case you're wondering how thin this is, it comes uncomfortably close to the weight criterion used by the American Psychiatric Association to diagnose anorexia nervosa (16 percent below ideal)! Fortunately, although extreme leanness is the basic body type in ballet, modern and Broadway dancers have more leeway, hovering around 6 percent below their ideal. This is a much more realistic goal for most women. Men, on the other hand, have less rigid standards to meet: They must just be muscular and look physically fit.

After looking at yourself in the mirror for years, it's easy to become your own worst critic. After all, whose body is perfect? In my *Dance Magazine* survey, only 23 percent of female dancers and 33 percent of male dancers said that they were satisfied with their bodies. In contrast, a British study of the general population found that over twice as many adolescent girls (47 percent) and boys (72 percent) were "satisfied." Though girls both in and out of dance seem to be most vulnerable to a negative body image, this is much more pronounced in dance.

### Are You Overweight?

When I asked this question to a large group of dancers who read *Dance Magazine*, I found that the ones whose weight fell within the normal or slightly above range for their height said yes; 37 percent were females and 11 percent were males. Many dancers get confused about where they stand in terms of their ideal weight. Here's a letter I received from a young dance student.

> *My recommended weight in population tables (published in the 1980s) is between 116 and 148 pounds. The problem is that I know ballerinas like Natalia Makarova, Cynthia Harvey, and Susan Jaffe each weighed (at that time) at least seven to nine pounds under the lowest weight in their height classification. This goal seems impossible to me, since I already watch what I eat and do aerobic exercise. I'm 15 years old. Help, please!"*

First of all, it's dangerous to judge yourself by others, because people carry their weight differently. It's also normal to gain weight as you mature. I know one fourteen-year-old girl whose weight crept up just before a growth spurt, while another teenager became a little plump as she went through puberty. Neither dancer ended up having a weight problem.

Presently, the Metropolitan Life Insurance Company's weight tables (1983) are being revised to reflect the lower weight tables of the past, because we now know that being thinner is actually healthier. While there's no such thing as a "magic number" on the scale, you can get a general idea of your weight by checking out Sargent's weight-height table (Table 3.1). I prefer using this table because, unlike other weight tables, the information comes from young adults, who were weighed without clothes and shoes.

To find out where you stand in relation to this table, divide your real weight by the ideal for your height and sex. For example, a female dancer five feet eight inches tall weighing 123 pounds can tell from Table 3.1 that she's 10 percent below her ideal weight for height. While this is within the normal range for most ballet dancers, remember that each dancer carries her weight differently. I know a dancer who's considered to be thin at five feet eight

**Table 3.1. Height-Weight Relationships.**

| Females | | Males | |
|---|---|---|---|
| Height | Weight (pounds) | Height | Weight (pounds) |
| 5' | 108 | 5'5" | 138 |
| 5'1" | 112 | 5'6" | 142 |
| 5'2" | 116 | 5'7" | 146 |
| 5'3" | 119 | 5'8" | 149 |
| 5'4" | 123 | 5'9" | 153 |
| 5'5" | 126 | 5'10" | 157 |
| 5'6" | 129 | 5'11" | 161 |
| 5'7" | 133 | 6' | 165 |
| 5'8" | 137 | 6'1" | 169 |
| 5'9" | 141 | 6'2" | 173 |
| 5'10" | 144 | 6'3" | 177 |
| 5'11" | 147 | 6'4" | 182 |

*Source:* Sargent, 1963, p. 321.

and a half inches, weighing in at 128 pounds, because she has big bones.

If you're a modern dancer, the weight requirements are less stringent, at 6 percent below ideal. In the previous example, this would amount to 129 pounds for a woman five feet eight inches tall. A male dancer in either style would normally hover a few pounds below his ideal weight of 149 pounds at the same height.

As you can see, weight can affect dancers' future prospects in the profession, as well as their body image and self-esteem. Though few dance schools have the financial means to offer nutritional counseling on a regular basis, educational seminars are a cost-effective way to help dancers achieve their goals. Unfortunately, only 31 percent of dancers in our national survey say that their dance school provides information on nutrition, and a mere 18 percent provide information on eating disorders. In the next section, we examine the price that dancers pay by taking matters into their own hands.

# How to Be Healthy and Thin

Over the years, I've heard from many desperate dancers, uninformed about the dangers of dieting, who decided to stop eating sugar, fat, meat, or anything at all. One twenty-year-old jazz student wrote to me about how she'd lived on a diet of grapefruit, cigarettes, and vitamin supplements until she fainted in class. I know another nineteen-year-old ballet student who became bulimic and gained twenty pounds after several months of following a menu limited to 800 calories a day. The worst case, however, was a lovely twenty-three-year-old girl who'd been starving herself since a school director told her to lose weight at the age of twelve. Injuries, muscle loss, and self-hate now made dancing an impossible dream. So before you start your next diet: Stop! It's time to find out why dieting causes more problems than it solves.

## What's Wrong with Dieting?

The answer is, a lot! Every time you take a drastic step to tip the scale, your body revs up to defend its natural weight against "attack." It's like having an internal thermostat that regulates weight instead of temperature. If your *set point*—the internal control mechanism that determines your weight—hovers at 130 pounds because of your genes, your body will do its best to keep you there by regulating your activity level, hunger, and metabolic rate. Dancers who ignore this fact get into trouble.

Unfortunately, many dancers who want to lose weight fast take extreme measures. One eighteen-year-old dancer stubbornly took this approach, eliminating necessary calories and fat. At first, she experienced a significant drop in energy, which led to a marked deterioration in performance. Over time, her reproductive functions also shut down: Whereas some dancers never start menstruating, this young woman stopped. The last straw occurred when she developed a stress fracture. Because estrogen was no longer there to keep the calcium in her bones, her bones became brittle, as in menopause!

She also was irritable and depressed, in some cases a response to starvation, which can even lead to psychotic levels of disorganization.

At this point I hear many dancers say, "I don't care how messed up my body gets, as long as I'm thin." The tragedy is that over time, dieting can actually make you fatter! Besides drastically increasing the urge to overeat, your body will fight you by slowing your resting metabolic rate as much as 45 percent, making losing weight increasingly difficult. If your hunger wins out, which is often the case, you'll gain a greater percentage of fat because muscle gain is very slow.

One twenty-five-year-old dancer repeated this cycle of weight loss and weight gain (known as the "yo-yo effect"). She would starve during the week, then binge on the weekend by eating everything in sight. Instead of losing weight, she started to gain it in leaps and bounds. At the end of the season, her director fired her. Can you guess why? It was for being overweight.

## Developing an Eating Disorder

Dancers who try to survive on caffeine and cigarettes are jeopardizing their health. An even more serious problem is a clinical eating disorder. Anorexia nervosa involves extreme weight loss, no menses for at least three months (amenorrhea), and the fear of becoming obese. In bulimia nervosa, secretive episodes of binge eating alternate with self-induced vomiting, fasting, compulsive exercise, or laxative or diuretic abuse. You should know that laxatives won't make you lose weight, whereas diuretics only affect water weight, which returns as soon as you begin eating and drinking. The dehydration that results from diuretics can also be dangerous. Besides decreasing muscle endurance and work capacity, diuretics cause you to lose electrolytes such as potassium and sodium, thus increasing the risk of cardiac arrythmias.

Binge-eating disorder, a new category used to describe people who binge without resorting to maladaptive ways to lose weight, is another serious problem. Let's look at some of the factors that play a big role in their occurrence.

People with eating disorders share several distorted attitudes, fostered by our culture's obsession with thinness. Here are some of the things they believe:

- Perfection is best, and any less means failure.

- Self-denial is always superior to self-indulgence.

- The most disgusting thing in the world is being fat.

- Gaining weight means a loss of control.

These rigid beliefs can tap into personal problems, to the point that being thin provides the illusion of escape. I know a leading dancer who thinks, "If I'm very, very thin, all of my problems will go away." In reality, she's struggling with feelings of inadequacy and low self-esteem. Three out of four people who develop a serious eating disorder are also depressed.

Dancers' outfits on any given day can indicate their mood and how they see themselves. I remember days when I used leg warmers, sweat pants, and baggy shirts to face the mirror when I was in a bad mood. Of course, there were also times when I felt confident and was happy to be seen in only a leotard and pink tights. Being depressed is different, because you feel as though you're stuck in quicksand. Your eating, sleep habits, attention, and hopefulness about the future are all impaired.

There are times when dancers are especially vulnerable to depression and disordered eating. One fifteen-year-old dancer who wrote to me developed an eating problem after a series of injuries kept her from class for over a year. She didn't have the right body for dance and began to compensate by dieting. Another twenty-three-year-old professional sought me out for psychotherapy when her friends became alarmed at her anorexia. She'd decided to switch dance companies six months prior to our meeting but had become overwhelmed by the competition. This reaction can also occur when talented dance students transfer to a more competitive school. One of the biggest problems, however, stems from teachers, directors, or critics who draw attention to the dancer's weight, leading to public humiliation.

## How Common Are Eating Disorders?

Young women are most likely to show signs of eating problems, from anorexic-like symptoms to serious disorders that require hospitalization. In the general population, the prevalence rate for anorexia nervosa affects about one out of every hundred, whereas bulimia nervosa occurs in up to 3 percent. It's rare for these problems to affect men, who make up only 5 to 10 percent of the new cases every year. In dance, as many as 46 percent of dancers report eating problems, although only 4 percent in my *Dance Magazine* survey actually met all of the diagnostic criteria for a clinical eating disorder. Take a moment to look over the American Psychiatric Association's official criteria for meeting anorexia nervosa:

### A Diagnosis of Anorexia Nervosa

1. Your weight is more than 15 percent below your ideal weight for height, or you fail to make expected weight gains while growing (use the table to see where you are).

2. You're underweight, but you have an intense fear of gaining weight or becoming fat.

3. You see yourself as fatter than you are, your appearance has too big an effect on your self-esteem, or you deny the seriousness of your current low weight.

4. You've missed at least three consecutive menstrual cycles, causing amenorrhea.

There are two types of anorexics: The *restricting anorexic* diets but doesn't binge or purge through vomiting, laxatives, diuretics, or enemas; the *binge-eating/purging anorexic* binges or purges regularly.

Anorexia nervosa is a serious problem than can play tricks with your mind as well as your body. I know one sixteen-year-old girl who acted as though she was in a hall of mirrors. She'd look at her body on one day and be thin. The next day, everything would change and all she saw was fat. No matter how much weight she lost, she'd always think, "I could lose a little bit more." This problem is extremely disconcerting to the people around you. Here's what one concerned dance teacher had to say.

> *I've been very worried lately about an adult student who*
> *takes my intermediate ballet class. She looks emaciated!*
> *I've spoken to her about her weight and even suggested that*
> *she get professional help. But nothing happens. I'm afraid*
> *that I'm contributing to the problem by letting her exercise.*

When in doubt, teachers can ask students for a letter from their physician stating that it's safe for them to take dance class at their present weight. Directors of schools and companies can also set a minimum dancing weight, such as 15 percent below ideal, to prevent severe emaciation. Dancers with eating disorders should always be followed by a physician and be referred for psychotherapy.

In my clinical practice, I've found that anorexics feel a great deal of pride over their self-control, which often makes them resistant to change. Over time, some of these dancers become bulimic. One twenty-four-year-old dancer in musical theater had been hospitalized for anorexia nervosa at sixteen. She continued to diet until going to college, where her eating pattern changed dramatically, leading to uncontrollable binges. By the time she came to see me, she was desperate to stop, which helped her prognosis considerably. Let's check out the following criteria for bulimics.

### A Diagnosis of Bulimia Nervosa

1. You binge within a two-hour period, eating a larger amount of food than others and feeling out of control.

2. You try to prevent weight gain by repeatedly vomiting or using other inappropriate means, including going overboard on exercise.

3. The bulimia is an ongoing problem: You binge or purge, on average, at least two times weekly and have done so for three months straight.

4. Your body shape and weight play a major role in your self-evaluation.

5. The bulimia doesn't occur only during an anorexic episode.

There are two types of bulimics: The *purging type* uses enemas, laxatives, vomiting, or diuretics to compensate for binge eating; the *nonpurging type* tries to compensate in other ways, such as with fasting or compulsive exercise.

As you can see, everyone with bulimia doesn't purge. However, nine out of ten bulimics do induce vomiting, which produces immediate relief from the physical discomfort of bingeing. The cost to your body can be astronomical. I know one forty-five-year-old dancer whose chronic vomiting removed the enamel from her teeth, disrupted her electrolyte balance, and ruptured her esophagus. Another retired dancer, who is now forty-four, can no longer have a normal bowel movement without help after taking thirty laxatives a day for the last two decades. The truth is that neither approach is particularly good at weight loss. Unfortunately, once you develop an eating disorder, it's usually very difficult to stop.

The last major eating problem described occurs in people who binge without compensating for those extra calories. As you'll see, this behavior is very similar to bulimia.

### Binge-Eating Disorder

1. As with bulimia nervosa, you have repeated binges within a two-hour period, where you eat a much larger amount of food than others and feel out of control.

2. Your binge has at least three of these characteristics:
   - You eat much more rapidly than usual.
   - You eat until you're uncomfortably full.
   - You overeat even when you aren't physically hungry.
   - You eat alone, embarrassed at the amount.
   - You feel disgusted, depressed, or guilty afterward.

3. Your problem with binge-eating makes you very unhappy.

4. This behavior is an ongoing problem: You binge two days a week and have done so for six months.

5. You don't try to compensate for your binge-eating in order to lose weight, and this problem isn't occurring only during an anorexic episode.

Binge-eating disorder is a common problem in women who attend weight-loss clinics for obesity, a finding that suggests that this problem occurs from fighting your genetic set point for weight. "Jane," a thirty-five-year-old recreational tap dancer, was fed up with being overweight, so she tried going on a liquid diet. Twelve months later, she came to see me because she now spent most of her day driving through every fast food restaurant in her neighborhood, wolfing down burgers, milkshakes, and apple pies. She had lost twenty pounds and gained back thirty more.

## How to Overcome Disorders

Eating disorders can ruin a dancer's life. If you are suffering from this problem, you can get help by calling the Renfrew Center (800-RENFREW) or your regional psychological association for a therapist who specializes in eating disorders. Dance schools and companies can also make changes to help prevent these problems. Dance teachers can help dancers (few of whom become professionals) by allowing for different sizes and shapes in class. Teachers and artistic directors can also refuse to give preferential treatment (such as a leading role) to dancers who are obviously emaciated. Finally, dancers should be offered educational seminars on eating disorders and healthy weight loss practices.

In the final section, I show you how to balance exercise, food intake, and temptation to achieve your optimal weight.

You *can* approach weight loss in a healthier way. To do this, you need to know how to burn calories, lower your set point through exercise, reduce your food intake without unleashing feelings of deprivation, and stick to a maintenance program. When the program is working, you'll know it, because it feels easy. Let's see how you can make a lifestyle change that works.

### Correct Exercise

An effective weight loss program rests on aerobic exercise, which is actually thought to lower your set point for weight. This type of exercise will affect your metabolic rate, since the energy generated by your muscles can increase nearly 120 times with vigorous exercise. In addition, regular aerobic exercise brings about enzymatic changes that facilitate fat metabolism while boosting your stamina.

A talented dancer from the School of American Ballet needed to lose five pounds for the annual workshop in which she had a leading role. Though her eating habits were good, weight problems ran in her family. To help her lower her set point, I recommended that she work out three to five times per week for thirty to forty-five minutes by biking, taking an aerobics class, or using the StairMaster. Swimming can also be good exercise, although there's some question about its increasing your appetite as a way to maintain fat insulation in cold water. This dancer lost the weight by using the stationary bike and was offered a position in a major ballet company.

Remember to choose an aerobic activity that places the least amount of stress on your body if you have a physical problem, such as a bad back. If you want to increase lean muscle, which is metabolically more active than fat, you can also incorporate weight-resistant exercise into your regime, such as the Pilates method, which emphasizes strength and flexibility within the dancer's turnout position.

## Eating Correctly

The next step for many dancers is to plan a balanced diet that includes a blend of carbohydrates, fat, and protein, as well as vitamins and minerals. At times, making the right choices can be confusing. Here's a question from a letter I got from one dancer.

> *What foods should be eaten before dance class, and which should be avoided?*

If you're going to lose weight the right way, you need to remember that you're an athlete as well as an artist. So before we go into the number of calories to eat, let's review the type of fuel that's right for you.

Because dancing isn't aerobic, all your zip comes from foods rich in carbohydrates, which are stored in your body in an energy form called glycogen. Glycogen stores are limited: The average amount of available energy is only about 200 calories. If you want to increase your muscles' capacity to store glycogen, add endurance training like swimming or the stationary bike. This form of exercise will use fat for fuel thirty to sixty minutes after you begin. Make 12 percent of your diet protein, since this is needed to repair tissue damaged during exercise. Avoid eating meat and other foods high in fat before you dance, as these are harder to digest.

I know one twenty-two-year-old modern dancer who went on a crash diet and began to show signs of glycogen depletion, including feelings of sluggishness, excessive fatigue, and "heavy" legs. To remedy this problem, I suggest eating unrefined or complex carbohydrates before you dance and replenishing your supplies afterward. Food choices include fruit, milk, yogurt, rice, breads, cereals, pasta, potatoes, peas, parsnips, sweet corn, dried beans, and lentils.

Many dancers are surprised to hear me say that complex carbohydrates should make up about 60 percent of a dancer's diet.

They've heard a lot of hoopla in the media about high-protein diets and negative comments about carbohydrates. However, these comments only apply to insulin-resistant dieters, who represent about 25 percent of the population and who tend to be overweight by normal standards—rarely the case for dancers. Dancers should also know that the body can lose lean muscle tissue on low-carbohydrate, high-protein diets, thus leading to fatigue and a reduction in metabolic rate.

## Intake of Fat and Calories

To reach your optimal low weight, daily food intake usually ranges between 1400–1600 calories for females and 1600–1800 calories for males, with 25 to 40 grams of fat. Dancers who are going through a growth spurt should aim for the higher number. Pamela Koch, the nutritionist at the School of American Ballet, often has erratic eaters adopt a lower caloric amount right away; but if you eat pretty much the same amount every day, she says that it's best to reduce your food intake slowly (about 300 calories every two weeks) so your body can adjust. Both approaches take a lot of discipline; the average dietary intake runs from 2200 to 2500 calories a day. Once you get to your optimal weight, add 100 calories every few days if your weight continues to drop.

The best way to maintain a high metabolic rate is to spread out your food intake over the day. If you decide to go in the other direction and starve, your body may eventually rebel, and you'll overeat. I worked with one twenty-six-year-old male dancer who was 5 percent above his ideal weight for height. He followed a meal plan that amounted to 1800 calories a day and 25 grams of fat. Along with using the stationary bike, this approach helped him to lose eight pounds.

Female dancers should also consume between 1200 and 1500 mg of calcium, whereas males need about 1000 mg daily. This helps to protect your bones, especially in females who are amenorrheic. All dancers should eat a balanced diet composed of calcium-rich foods, because no food group will give you all the calcium you need. For example, plant-based foods, such as leafy green vegetables, legumes, broccoli, and figs, are good sources of calcium but difficult for the body to absorb. Dairy products, on the other hand, are more readily absorbed, although too much protein will cause you to lose calcium through your urine. Caffeine and colas can also deplete your body of calcium.

A final word for women about amenorrhea. Once you stop menstruating, you may lose about 4 percent of your bone mass annually for the next three to four years before this process slows down to a lower rate. This can lead to stress fractures and osteoporosis (loss of bone density) in later life, similar to going through menopause. Besides telling dancers to pay attention to diet and use calcium supplements, I advise them to see an endocrinologist if this problem continues past six months. Dr. Michelle Warren, the medical director of the Center for Menopause, Hormonal Disorders, and Women's Health in New York City, often recommends going on a low dosage of estrogen-replacement therapy to induce menstruation and protect your skeletal system. Taking the pills won't make you gain weight, but it may help your bones!

Of course, this is easier said than done if you're also struggling with anorexia nervosa. As I mentioned earlier in the section on hormonal functioning, amenorrhea is one of the consequences of severe weight loss. In girls who have yet to menstruate, anorexia can delay menarche. I'm currently treating a twenty-year-old anorexic dancer with primary amenorrhea (she's never menstruated). So far, I've succeeded in getting her to an endocrinologist, who put her on a very low dose of estrogen-replacement therapy, which may offer some protection for her bones. Yet this dancer currently refuses to increase the dosage and face the onset of being a woman.

Dancers without eating disorders can usually make the necessary changes in food and exercise. Remember, a balanced diet includes a variety of healthy foods that are low in fat and rich in vegetables, fruits, and complex carbohydrates. Vitamin supplements are necessary only if you have a deficiency; high doses can be dangerous. Still, juggling all of your nutritional needs can be confusing even for an underweight dancer who wants to gain weight. If you need more information, contact the Nutrition Hotline (800–366–1655) sponsored by the American Dietetic Association. This service can refer you to a registered sport dietician in your area, and provide you with free nutritional information over the phone.

Although the obvious goal is to eat right, you can give in to temptation once in a while. The following letter is from a young dancer who thought she had to be perfect.

> *I like to eat all the usual American junky sorts of foods like cheeseburgers, fries, chocolate, colas, and so on. But when I'm older I want to become a professional dancer. Can you give me some typical dancer (healthy) types of foods and some suggestions on how to stick with them?*

Believe it or not, it's OK to eat a cheeseburger—once in a while—because it is the amount of calories you eat over the entire week, not in one meal, that's going to affect your weight. Unfortunately, dancers often get into trouble by going overboard. I know one fifteen-year-old ballet student who believed that she had to cut out all junk food. She managed to last until going to the neighborhood mall with her girlfriends, when she went overboard on ice cream and candy.

It's best to strike a balance. Choose foods that you like, so it'll be easier to stick with your meal plan—and feel free to add in low-fat desserts! If you're looking for super food choices with the highest nutritional potency, pick any of the following: almonds, dried apricots, cantaloupe, carrots, oat cereals, tofu, cabbage, sunflower seeds, tuna fish, yogurt, broccoli, salmon, sweet potatoes, milk, oysters, and wheat germ. Remember: Habits are often difficult to change, so give yourself time to adjust.

### Results to Aim For

A sensible approach, using exercise and a smart meal plan, can lead to weight loss amounting to one or two pounds a week. Sometimes, though, I have to caution dancers to stop weighing themselves every day. This was the case for one overeager twenty-year-old soloist in a ballet company who would weigh herself three times a day and become alarmed as the number changed due to water weight. Weekly weigh-ins—never daily!—will give you an accurate idea of your progress.

It's also important to be patient. Dancers who give up after only a couple of weeks remain frustrated, because short periods of dieting affect your body's carbohydrate stores and result primarily in water loss. It will take three weeks before 85 percent of your lost weight is body fat. Meanwhile, it's important to drink a lot of water—up to eight glasses is recommended—to prevent dehydration.

What can you expect? Dancers who reduce their daily food intake by only 100 calories while increasing their energy expenditure by the same amount (the equivalent of jogging daily for one mile) should lose twenty-one pounds in one year. Obviously, this example is meant to illustrate how effective a sensible approach can be, since most dancers wouldn't need to lose this much weight.

If you decide to go off your meal plan on a special occasion, aim mostly for food that contains low dietary fat (because high-fat foods are more easily converted to body fat, some weight-loss specialists believe). Low-fat substitutes, such as frozen yogurt or turkey burgers, can be just as satisfying. But don't eliminate all fat; it's an important nutrient and slows the rate of digestion.

### Changing Specific Body Parts

Many of the questions that I receive through my advice column ask if it's possible to reduce fat selectively at a specific site by "spot" reducing. This is hard to do, because the number of fat cells is fixed, so you can only reduce weight as a whole.

There's also nothing you can do to make cellulite disappear completely. A common misperception is that cellulite is composed of a different type of fat, containing toxins that the body has failed to eliminate. This is simply not true. Heredity, weight, and age create cellulite when pockets of ordinary fat push out between fibers connecting your skin to underlying tissues. Wrapping your body in seaweed or plastic, taking nutritional supplements, getting liposuction, or using spot reducers won't get rid of that orange-peel look. The only way to *minimize* those dimples is to lose excess weight.

Breast size is also a concern for certain dancers; 16 percent of dancers have opted for cosmetic surgery. One dissatisfied twenty-six-year-old dancer wrote to me after reducing the size of her breasts. Though she looked fine in a leotard, the scars (which are unpredictable with this operation) were quite prominent without clothes. At times, surgeons use liposuction to minimize scarring when the breasts are composed of a high percentage of fat and the nipples are level with the breast crease. Still, there's always a risk of complications (infection, bleeding, numbness), and vigorous exercise isn't possible for at least three weeks. A better approach is to try a special bra used by companies like the New York City Ballet to create a more linear look (see the Resource Directory).

## Making a Lifestyle Change

Your ability to keep weight off will depend on how well you adjust to a maintenance program. If bad eating habits have become a big part of your life, you might consider joining a support group or program such as Weight Watchers. Remember, it's normal to experience plateaus and setbacks, particularly if you eat for emotional reasons.

By the time many dancers contact me because of weight problems, they're often discouraged. They believe, "I'll never get my body to change." I'm here to tell you that it's possible to get better results if you work with—rather than against—your body. Exercise, combined with a sensible dietary plan, is the most effective approach to weight loss. Although you can't force your body to look like someone else's, you can make a significant difference—as long as you're realistic.

———————

In the next chapter, we look at the relationships that develop both inside and outside of dance. Because it's common to spend most of your time working with other dancers, the dance world often feels like one big family. Yet your friends can also be your competitors, making relationships hard to keep. Teasing and jealousy from non-dancers, as well as the hidden topic of sexual harassment, are additional problems that need to be addressed. Let's find out how to manage these pitfalls without becoming isolated from others.

# $\mathcal{Y}$our Relationships

## *Friends or Foes?*

$\mathcal{D}$ancing may be your life, but it's lonely if all you have is your dance bag for company. Unfortunately, dancers, both young and old, often find that dancing gets in the way of friendships, marriage, and starting a family. Many frustrated dancers ask me, "Will I ever have a personal life?"

Though you *can* develop close relationships and be a dancer, it helps to be aware of the interpersonal stresses in the profession. In this chapter, I explore how to get along with others by understanding the pressures around making friends while dealing with competition, teasing, and scheduling demands; handling the dating scene and your emerging sexuality; and protecting yourself in the face of sexual harassment.

## A Family Affair

The dance world often resembles a close-knit family in which you and your "siblings" (other dancers) compete for roles, promotions, and—I'm sorry to say—being the thinnest dancer in the class. Over the years I've gotten letters from young dancers whose friendships became strained by a constant push to be the best.

Making friends outside of dance is also challenging, especially in adolescence. Just when teenagers need to fit in with their peers, you're stuck with being different, from your turnout or hair bun to your never-ending schedule of dance classes. Fortunately, there are strategies to handle these conflicts. So, let's take a closer look at what can get between you and your friends.

**Competition Between Dancers**

Even though competition is a fact of life in dance, some of my best friends have been dancers. We became close by taking classes and rehearsals together, commiserating over sore toes and pulled muscles, and performing ballets onstage. The hard part was feeling jealous if one person received better roles than the other. Mostly, we kept these feelings to ourselves. Here's a letter from a fifteen-year-old dancer who experienced the same problem.

> I plan to pursue a career in ballet. The only problem is that my best friend, who is a year younger, has the same plans. Every time I think I've done something well, she does it better. I love her to death but this jealousy is killing me.

A common trap in dance is to compare yourself to others. You worry, "Is my friend a better dancer than I am?" Yet dancers improve at different rates. For example, tall dancers take more time to mature because longer limbs are harder to control. Differences in kinesthetic ability and anatomy will also affect your technical development. So if you're constantly evaluating yourself against other dancers, it's easy to feel upset.

A more constructive approach is to learn from other dancers while accepting the fact that you're all different. I know a twenty-five-year-old professional dancer who was unable to compete on a technical level with her friends, many of whom were performing solo roles. Instead of becoming jealous, she continued to support them while developing her own dramatic capacity, where her real talent lay. Now, her friends are helping her to get better roles by being supportive and boosting her morale, in turn.

But what happens if the competition keeps you from making friends in the first place? A sixteen-year-old boy wrote to me for advice after he went to a new dance studio and landed the leading part in the annual workshop. Suddenly the other top dancer at the school saw him as a rival and began turning the rest of the dancers against him. Under these circumstances, it's easy to say to yourself, "Who needs friends anyway?" Yet this will only make matters worse by leaving you all alone. What can this boy do?

There are several strategies to improve the situation. First, this dancer could mingle with the other dancers after class so they get to know him. Next, he could make a point of joining casual groups going out for lunch. The final step would be to invite the dancers he's comfortable with over to his house, perhaps to watch videos. The more familiar he becomes to everyone, the less likely they are to view him as the enemy. Of course, if the situation deteriorates, he should speak to his teacher. It takes more than one person to improve a relationship.

## Teasing from Nondancers

I know some dancers who believe that the best way to avoid personal conflicts is to make friends with people outside of dance. After all, you don't have to worry about competing for the same roles, and no one is sizing you up to see whether you're "dancer-thin." The problem here is that you may get teased for standing out from the crowd, because you're a dancer. Here are some examples of being teased:

- "She's stuck-up 'cause she won a competition."

- "Look at the surfboard with the flat chest."

- "Only guys who're sissies take ballet."

- "Hey, weirdo, you walk like a duck."

- "Where's your tutu, fairy?"

Boys often get the brunt of teasing; many kids think that dancing is only for girls. The next letter comes from a male dancer who wrote to me about this problem.

> I've danced for many years. But then I entered high school, and my problems began. The guys here think dance is for weenies. I know it isn't true and I tell them that, but they still tease me about it. This makes me feel really bad. I love dance. Yet I also need some friends. What should I do?

Obviously, these guys have never taken a ballet class. If they had, they would know that dancing is hard work. A classic study by Dr. James Nicholas at Lenox Hill Hospital in New York City found that ballet is more physically and mentally demanding than sixty sports, including professional football and hockey! Perhaps his friends will see the light. One reformed bully told me that he used to tease a male cousin about his dancing until the unimaginable happened: He had a growth spurt and his gym teacher suggested that *he* take dance classes, because he was so uncoordinated. This young man now believes that dancing helped him to become a leader rather than a follower, eventually winning him the Rotary Youth Leadership Award.

While stepping away from the crowd is risky, the payoff for being true to yourself is self-respect. Of course, you still may take some flak from your peers. So, what can you do? One approach is to educate your friends about dancing by inviting them over to your house to see *The Turning Point*, which showcases the fantastic technique of Baryshnikov, or by going to see a live performance onstage. If they continue to tease you, laugh it off—or look bored. Teasing is only fun if it gets a strong reaction. The good news is that once you become an adult, your friends are more likely to appreciate you for being special.

## Scheduling Demands

Dancing is a life based on discipline and hard work, hardly the normal state of affairs for a teenager. As your training becomes more advanced, there may be even less time to hang out and relax. Of course, if you love to dance more than anything, it's also time well spent. Is it possible to find a balance between work and having friends?

"Debbie," a twenty-three-year-old performer in a ballet company, fell into a typical dancer's rut. Like many serious dancers, she would work on her technique all day before collapsing each night in exhaustion. Her one day off was spent doing necessary but tedious errands like her laundry. By the end of the season, she often complained of feeling lonely and depressed. Debbie didn't know that the best antidote to burnout is having fun. Instead, she believed that a true dancer should put work above everything else.

Dancers who immerse themselves in work often have trouble handling stress; a missed double pirouette or a minor injury seems catastrophic. After enough time, dancing can feel more like a job than a joy. I know a twenty-seven-year-old modern dancer who finally discovered that she could socialize and have hobbies without interfering with her progress in dance. In fact, these activities gave her additional ways of feeling good about herself, helping to bolster her during periods of stress. I often advise dancers to add fun activities with a friend to each week. Many things are outside of our control. Fortunately, coping isn't one of them.

As you can see, friendships are not only possible but helpful. Besides giving your life in dance some balance and preventing burnout, relationships make it easier to cope with problems. This is especially important as you become more independent from your family of origin and enter the often tumultuous world of dating.

## Dating and Sexuality

Most teenagers are interested in going out on dates. Yet sometimes dancers are slow to hop on the bandwagon. What makes dancers hold back from forming intimate relationships?

Certainly, finding a date is difficult in dance class. Besides the focus being on work rather than play, girls can outnumber boys twenty to one. Yet it's also rare for dancers to mix with their school-mates in extracurricular activities like cheerleading or sports, be-cause of time constraints and the danger of athletic injuries.

One seventeen-year-old dancer attended the Professional Chil-dren's School in New York City, because it allowed him to break for a morning dance class, return to school, then head out for another dance class. By the time he finished his homework, it was time for bed. While this dancer did hang out occasionally with his friends, there wasn't much time to flirt.

Yet another reason for dancers' monastic existence has to do with hormones. As you may recall, dancers often have a delay in puberty from their intense exercise, diets, and low weights. My re-search shows that girls with delayed breast and pubic development are less interested in romance than those who develop at the av-erage time. I know a nineteen-year-old dancer whose younger sis-ter was bugging her about being dateless. Unlike her sibling, who had a boyfriend, this dancer had yet to menstruate and had no in-terest in dating. Her problem, as she saw it, was getting her sister off her back, because she was perfectly content to daydream about ballet.

A final obstacle to intimacy in dance is being married to your work. I know a number of teenagers—and some adults—who firmly insist, "Dating will only distract me from my dancing." Yet, even when you aren't looking for true love, Cupid's arrow may strike at any time. This teenage dancer wrote to me in a panic after discov-ering her knight in shining armor:

*Help! I've fallen in love with the Nutcracker Prince. I'm dancing the role of Clara with the same partner that I've had for the last three years. Now I've developed this crush on him that I can't hide. I know it's affecting my dancing. How can I stop thinking that I love him?*

While it's hard simply to *stop* those feelings, they don't have to interfere with your dancing, as long as you continue to take class. In fact, I know one twenty-four-year-old principal dancer who channeled her newfound feelings into her performances, especially of *Romeo and Juliet*. By the end of the season, she had a pile of rave reviews for an extra special dimension in her dancing. Of course, if it's simply an infatuation—and not true love—you could be back to normal in as little as six weeks. Your dancing, however, can reap long-term benefits.

A different type of problem occurs when teachers or directors disapprove of your love interest, because they want you all to themselves. Mr. Balanchine, my former director at New York City Ballet, was known to get extremely upset at many of his favorite female dancers if they found boyfriends. Here's what one twenty-six-year-old soloist said about this director during our interview:

*We dancers all knew that we should leave our boyfriends three blocks away and then walk to the theater. And no kissing on the streets! God forbid if you're met at the stage door. Anyway, I did all that but he still found out from one of the other dancers that I was involved with this guy. He was furious and started taking me out of ballets. I was devastated. Then, I got resentful and started to overeat. I know it was childish but I wanted to punish him. It didn't work. I just ended up gaining weight and becoming even more unhappy because I was punishing myself.*

Although this case is an extreme example, I still hear of directors who react badly when their favorites develop an intimate relationship or start a family. The irony is that many dancers perform better after they've established a fulfilling life outside of dance. Lourdes Lopez, a former ballerina with the New York City Ballet, traces the birth of her first child to a deepening artistry onstage, after Peter Martins became the ballet master in chief. (Day care, however, is still up to you. To my knowledge, the Alvin Ailey American Dance Company is the only performing arts group in the United States that provides some on-site child care to its members, through its affiliation with a performing arts union.)

Of course, even when your director doesn't mind if you have a life, dating someone in the same dance company is a mixed blessing. The benefits come from being with someone who shares your schedule and understands the pressures of the profession. The difficulty occurs if the relationship doesn't work out. One distraught dancer wrote to me, asking for help after a particularly upsetting break-up:

> A few weeks ago I broke up with my boyfriend. We're both in the same dance company and it's torture to see him with his new girlfriend every day. The worst part is that everyone knows.

Following the end of a relationship, you're often in a difficult position, because there's no such thing as privacy inside a dance company. Rejection is a blow to anyone's self-esteem. When it happens in front of your colleagues, it can seem even more humiliating. Your first priority after a break-up must be your own well-being. It's often possible to get some comfort from focusing on your dancing; however, you'll also need a lot of emotional support. Friends can be of enormous help; this isn't the time to be isolated from others. Try to be gentle with yourself; don't focus on what you may have done. The reasons that relationships end are often complex.

After you've gotten over the initial shock, you can reevaluate what went wrong and try to learn something from the experience.

Another problem that gets in the way of intimacy occurs because of dancers' work schedules, especially tours. Here's a letter from a dancer who found herself in this awkward predicament:

> Last fall I married a wonderful man. Everything was perfect, except that I didn't have a job. A month ago I was accepted into a modern dance company, and I thought my problem was solved. Boy, was I wrong! A tour is coming up, and my husband looks miserable. We're also fighting nonstop. Is it going to be like this every time I go away?

Touring may be a fact of life for dancers, but that doesn't mean it's easy. It requires a major adjustment, particularly if your spouse stays home. Let's face it, separations are difficult. A tour brings you face-to-face with your own insecurities and shows you just how much you can trust that other person. While it's natural to be irritated and tense, quarreling won't help. Communicating will, as long as you keep your tempers and try to establish some ground rules. It's also important to maintain contact while you're apart. The phone bills will be worth it.

If you're considering embarking on a close relationship, your sexual orientation will also play a role in the choice of a mate. Are dancers similar to the general population? Let's take a look.

## Sexual Orientation

When I asked about sexual interests in the *Dance Magazine* survey, I learned that 50 percent of men and 96 percent of women describe themselves as heterosexual; 2 percent (all females) say they're asexual. Men show the greatest difference in terms of same-sex preference: the 50 percent of male dancers who define themselves as homosexual or bisexual compares to 3 percent of men in the general population. The incidence of same-sex preference is 2 percent in female dancers, compared to 1 percent among women in general. Since men show the most variation in sexual orientation, we should consider what's it like to be a male in dance.

Like all dancers, boys gravitate to dance because of their interest in this art form. Exactly how you become homosexual or heterosexual isn't known. Still, experts agree that sexual preferences are fixed early in life (between ages two and four), with the best predictor of sexual orientation being your childhood play preferences.

For example, were you a boy who liked rough-and-tumble games with other boys, or did you prefer playing house with girls? I know one twenty-one-year-old gay man who loved to play dress-up with his sister, while his brothers were out playing baseball. Although some experts debate whether cross-gender behavior is part of a pre-homosexual pattern, the prevailing belief is that the more extensive this behavior is during childhood, the more likely you will be gay, especially for males.

Being different from other children is never easy, as you'll see in this next letter from a young dancer:

> I'm a boy. For Halloween I lost a bet to my sister and she got to choose how I would dress up—as a ballerina! The weirdest thing is how I felt in tights and a tutu. I've already been a ballerina in secret when no one is home. Now I wonder how my sister's other clothes would feel. Is there something wrong with me? If I start ballet, will these feelings go away or get worse? I don't know how my parents would react. Please help! I'm twelve years old.

Right now, this boy is feeling very confused. If he keeps his concerns to himself, he may become isolated and develop low self-esteem. It's important to reach out for help, preferably from your mother if you're a child. Ballet won't make these feelings worse. But it isn't the answer either.

As we've already discussed, cross-gender behavior doesn't always mean that you'll grow up gay. I often receive letters from parents who are concerned that dance will cause their young boys to become homosexuals. There's nothing in the research to suggest that this is true. In fact, sexual attraction, sexual activity, and sexual identity are fairly independent. For example, research shows that teenagers who have an experience with a same-sex partner may not identify themselves as gay. It's also possible to be attracted to someone without acting upon it. Sexual orientation, on the other hand, is a complex process of development mostly under internal control.

Still, if you do find that you're gay, adjusting to this during adolescence is never easy. Even though homosexuality may have lost some of its stigma over the last two decades, 67 percent of American adults continue to view it as "always wrong," according to an extensive National Health and Social Life Survey released in 1994. In contrast, the dance world's reaction to same-sex preferences is generally favorable, offering a degree of social acceptance that's often lacking in today's society. The straight male is the one who may feel defensive in dance, because others may assume that he's gay. I know one twenty-three-year-old male dancer who deals with this issue by trying to prove his masculinity: He acts macho and dates a lot of women.

So far, we've been discussing the bumpy but exciting world of dating, falling in love, and making a commitment to another person. Although more dancers are developing personal lives than ever before, there's still lots of room for improvement. Though certain impediments, like busy work schedules and delayed maturity, are unlikely to change, there's no need to sacrifice intimate relationships to excel in this profession. With the right approach, striking a balance between personal and professional needs is possible. Yet there is another type of relationship that often gets confused with intimacy: sexual harassment. Someone wants you—but you don't want them.

## Being Sexually Harassed

Dance brings to mind many things—physicality, grace, perhaps even a more enlightened way of life. It's a world based on hard work and dedication, in which the pursuit of perfection is the rule. In fact, the dance world is about as far away from real-life problems like sexual harassment as you can get, right?

It depends on whom you believe. According to a lawsuit filed in 1995, sexual misconduct between certain dance faculty members and students at the North Carolina School of the Arts was common knowledge. The charges were made by a former modern dancer, who alleged that he was seduced by his teacher into a sexual relationship at the age of sixteen, with the *encouragement* of another teacher and the knowledge of school officials. Both teachers, well known and respected in the dance world, denied the allegations but have since resigned, stating that their credibility had been undermined. The dancer subsequently dropped the suit against the school, although charges against the teachers are still pending.

Whether or not the accusations are true, I believe that dancers need to be prepared to handle real-life situations in addition to their *battements* and *tendues*. This section tells you about sexual harassment in dance and how to deal with it if it should happen to you.

### What Is Sexual Harassment?

Any form of unwanted sexual attention, whether verbal or physical, is considered harassment, particularly in a relationship of unequal power. Criminal charges encompass a variety of the most serious areas, such as assault, battery, and rape. In addition, sex between a minor (under eighteen years old) and an adult is always illegal, whether or not the minor consents.

Dancers need to understand that sexual harassment has very little to do with sex. Instead, the perpetrator often uses it to express hostility or anger, or as a way to show power or to compensate for a deficiency in power. I know a nineteen-year-old dancer who told me about an aging teacher (now retired) who would constantly intimidate her by making demeaning sexual comments in her presence. Another male dancer felt pressured to date an older dancer in his company, because of this man's stature.

Because young dancers often don't understand the concept of consent, they may blame themselves for submitting to the harasser or for becoming aroused. Guilt is also an issue for adult victims who experience "frozen fright," a reaction of pure terror that temporally disables them at the moment when they might be expected to ask for help. Finally, it's almost universal that sexual harassment will cause victims to experience feelings of shame and humiliation. Victims must remember that it is their sexual harassers—not themselves—who are wrong. Self-blame only makes matters worse.

Dancers should know that sex under the age of eighteen is illegal, even if it is consensual. Examples of nonconsensual sex with someone after this age include activities that are unwelcome, make you feel personally violated, or keep you from feeling free to stop. In the case of the North Carolina School of the Arts (NCSA), the charge of flagrant sex between faculty and students has lead to a sexual harassment policy that now prohibits consensual sexual relations when an employee is responsible for evaluating or supervising a student or if the student is a minor.

Dancers should also be aware of certain behaviors that aren't considered sexual harassment. These include a single unwelcome request for a date, an isolated case of sexual teasing or gender-related jokes, or occasional instances of an instructor or student pressing against another student as they pass each other in the hallway.

Other areas in dance are a bit more ambiguous. For example, a twenty-five-year-old professional ballet dancer told me that she had stopped going to a massage therapist after he had removed her towel and begun to massage the top of her breasts; her friends, however, continued to see this masseur and let him remove their towels, making my client wonder if she was inhibited. A year later, she returned to him, stated her reservations but allowed him to discuss sex with her during the massage. This dancer said that she knew it was only a matter of time before he would remove her towel again. She just hoped that she would be able to accept it.

I believe that this is a classic example of sexual harassment. It is unwanted, unnecessary, and makes my client feel pressured into going along with something that doesn't feel right. The tragedy is that most dancers jump to the conclusion that they're the ones with a problem rather than placing the blame on their abuser.

Another confusing area in dance involves teachers who use sexual terms to describe certain movements, such as a Graham contraction. While some teachers may believe such terminology is essential to the art form, students should feel free to ask their teachers to stop such references (as well as any other verbal comments that smack of abuse) if they find such terms upsetting. Diane Gray, the former director of the Martha Graham School and former associate director of the company, advises institutions to check the backgrounds of guest teachers and choreographers thoroughly before inviting them to their schools. Both verbal abuse and sexual harassment tend to recur repeatedly over time.

Finally, the "hands-on" approach used by many dance teachers to correct alignment may be experienced differently by different students, depending on their background and their zone of comfort with the instructor. To avoid confusion, Janet Hamburg, the former director of the University of Kansas dance department, advised students at the onset of each school year to let their teachers know if they found it disturbing and did not want to be touched.

## How Common Is Sexual Harassment?

This problem usually begins in schools, where children and young adults spend most of their time. According to the results from a national survey compiled by the New York State Coalition Against Sexual Assault, one in every four schoolgirls and one in every six schoolboys will be sexually assaulted by age eighteen. Furthermore, approximately 85 percent of victims of sexual assault know their attackers.

Like other students, dancers spend considerable time in school over a period of years in the company of their peers, where teasing and sexual stereotyping are common. They're also influenced by their relationships with school officials, who occupy positions of power and trust in their lives. A teacher's yearly evaluations, suggestions for promotions, and letters of recommendation will be crucial to a dancer's career. None of these dynamics necessarily predict sexual harassment; however, problems may arise if dancers feel pressured to please, to fit in with their peers, or to avoid conflicts that might endanger their future aspirations.

Keeping this in mind, I asked three hundred dancers in a national survey if they had ever been sexually harassed in dance. Sixteen percent said yes to one or more scenarios typical of sexual harassment. The biggest surprise involves the men, who turn out to be the most common targets of harassment in their late teens. The ratio of male to female harassers is seven to one.

As Table 4.1 shows, three times more male than female dancers are the recipients of explicit sexual comments. This behavior comes mainly from male artistic directors and choreographers—authority figures who hold dancers' careers in the balance. Only 5 percent of these harassers are female. Male dancers are also more likely to be propositioned for sex than females by a variety of men in the dance world.

Among the female dancers, I found that those who have to fend off repeated requests for a date by other students suffer from a more negative body image compared to females who aren't harassed. Furthermore, inappropriate touching by their dance teachers is related to a diagnosis of a clinical eating disorder. Female dancers who've been forcibly grabbed, hugged, and kissed by other students are less likely to practice safe sex. So, while girls are less likely to be harassed in dance than they are in regular school, the problems associated

Table 4.1. Sexual Harassment in the Dance World.

| Someone: | Harassed Females (percent) | Who?[a] | Harassed Males (percent) | Who?[a] | Gender of Harasser (percent)[b] |
|---|---|---|---|---|---|
| Made explicit sexual comments over time | 6 | Teacher | 22 | Director or choreographer | M (65), F (5) |
| Propositioned you for sex | 5 | Student | 17 | All | M (69), F (19) |
| Forcibly hugged, grabbed, or kissed you | 5 | Student | 11 | Student | M (47), F (7) |
| Touched you in dance, unrelated to corrections | 4 | Teacher | 6 | Student | M (58), F (17) |
| Group made sexual comments or asked you to have sex as you passed by | 3 | Students | 0 | N/A[c] | M (56), F (0) |
| Asked repeatedly for a date with you despite your lack of interest | 2 | Student | 0 | N/A | M (57), F (0) |
| Forced you to have sex | 1 | Other | 0 | N/A | M (33), F (0) |

[a]The choices were *student, teacher, director, choreographer,* or *other person in the dance world.*

[b]M = male, F = female; percentages do not add up to 100 because some dancers left the gender of the perpetrator blank.

[c]N/A = not applicable.

with these behaviors are severe. Here's a letter from a young girl
who found herself struggling with this problem in dance class:

> *I'm a sixteen-year-old girl and my favorite class used to be*
> *partnering. That is, until I started to be sexually harassed*
> *by just about every guy in the class. The directors know but*
> *do nothing about it. Yet the school is one of the best. Help!*

Ignoring sexual harassment will not end it! Forty-six percent of
victims use this strategy, but only one in four actually succeeds in
getting the harasser to stop. Here are some effective suggestions.

1.  Learn to say no. Your voice is a powerful tool. Pay attention
when you bodily sensations alert you to behavior that causes fear,
discomfort, or confusion. Tell your harasser that you find the behavior offensive; do *not* be apologetic. You are the one who is being
harassed.

2.  Make eye contact, keep your voice firm, and try to be as confident as possible. If you're nervous, perhaps you should rehearse this
approach with a friend. However, if you are still too uncomfortable,
write a polite but factual letter to your harasser explaining how you
feel about the event and what you want to happen next. Again, it
helps to have a second opinion. Deliver the letter in person or by
certified mail, and keep a copy for yourself.

3.  Report the misconduct to a school official. Ideally, your
school will have a sexual harassment and counseling policy, with a
"safe contact person" who's expert in handling this problem. To be
effective, as well as to protect schools from liability, this policy
should include a grievance procedure with formal and informal avenues of redress to encourage victims to come forward. A specific
policy on sexual harassment should list penalties that the school
can levy against the harasser; it should also state penalties for filing
false complaints.

4. Keep a journal that lists the time, date, and place of each occurrence; any witnesses to the event; and as much detail as possible. Describe the harasser's words and actions and how they made you feel. Include their impact on your health and school performance.

5. If the behavior continues after you have contacted school officials, file a formal complaint at the school. You also have six months (except under unusual circumstances) to file a discrimination complaint with the state office for civil rights or the U.S. Department of Education or to bring a lawsuit.

Professionals who suspect that a minor has been sexually abused are required by law to report the event to a child protection agency. One teacher I know from NCSA felt bad that she hadn't checked out the rumors of sexual goings-on between faculty and students. In addition, teachers and parents should check with other parents before assuming that this is an isolated event.

## Your Reaction to Trauma

People who are traumatized often detach themselves emotionally, physically, and intellectually from the event. I know one eighteen-year-old female dancer who was raped by the brother of another dance student. Over the next few days, she experienced an intense stress reaction, with disturbances in both psychological and physical functioning. Emotionally, it can feel as though you're on a roller coaster. From moment to moment you may find yourself switching from rage to helplessness or from composure to terror. Somatic complaints are also common, including nausea, trembling, headaches, and insomnia.

Though few dancers have to contend with rape (only 1 percent in the previous survey were forced to have sex), any sexual contact that's nonconsensual can be traumatic, so it's essential to get immediate medical attention within the first seventy-two hours. Call a rape crisis center and have an advocate present at the hospital, even if an incomplete sexual assault has occurred. Crisis interventions, including supportive psychotherapy, are also helpful during the initial stages of recovery.

Unfortunately, victims of trauma often experience a number of potential symptoms for years without receiving treatment. For example, you may feel intense fear in situations similar to the abusive event. Flashbacks, intrusive thoughts, and nightmares can also occur. Whereas flashbacks can be frightening, they also give you an opportunity to express the initial terror that may not have been possible during the assault. In contrast, nightmares interfere with sleep and recovery, and temporary medication from a physician may be needed to reduce your anxiety.

During this time, you may find yourself engaging in unusual behaviors such as compulsive bathing, eating, or drinking to regain emotional control. I worked with one twenty-one-year-old modern dancer who was fondled sexually during a physical therapy session by someone with a lot of clients in the dance world. At the time, she experienced "frozen fright," leaving her guilt-ridden and confused. During the next few weeks, she suffered numerous migraine headaches, as well as episodes of bingeing, followed by self-induced vomiting. She was unable to take dance class and fell into a deep depression. This pattern is consistent with a diagnosis of posttraumatic stress disorder, when your reactions deviate from normal behavior and cause significant distress or impairment in social, work-related, or other important areas of functioning. By giving this dancer a lot of support, I was able to help her get through this period. We both celebrated on the day that she testified against this man in court.

A period of relative calm can occur for some traumatized people after the first six weeks. This may seem confusing to family members and friends. However, it is a necessary part of the healing process, similar to encasing a broken leg in a cast. At this point, many victims refuse to discuss the sexual abuse, decide to leave psychotherapy, or move to another state. This is only a temporary resolution. Frequently, symptoms return when the victim is better prepared to deal with them. I know one thirty-year-old dancer who is just now dealing with being attacked by another dancer on tour when she was in her teens. The fact is that posttraumatic stress reaction may reappear months or even years after the trauma.

### What the Dance World Can Do

Sexual harassment is viewed by the courts as a serious violation of the Equal Rights Act of 1964 and the Fourteenth Amendment to the Constitution of the United States. Currently, a school can be held liable for all types of problems in this area, including those generated from student to student. A school policy should offer protection and help you establish the truth, while guarding against frivolous or malicious charges brought against students, employees, or faculty members. Dance schools can find out more about setting up a sexual harassment and counseling policy by reading the handbook by Shoop and Edwards listed in the Further Reading section. Dance companies should also have specific procedures to protect members and any children who perform in their productions.

Education doesn't create more sexual harassment. Instead, it gives a name to inappropriate behaviors that may already exist in the performing arts. Remember: If you have been sexually harassed, do not blame yourself. Do not delay. Do not keep quiet! You may not be the only victim.

## Creating Relationships

The ultimate value and importance of relationships lies in their ability to bridge the gap between you and other people. When I was a dancer, I remember being told that marriage was taboo and that even having a cat would detract from my work. I now know that this kind of sacrifice isn't necessary. In fact, research shows that besides adding to the quality of our lives, close relationships actually contribute to our longevity! I believe that your dancing can also improve. Here are two role models for the current generation of dancers.

Darci Kistler is a ballerina in the New York City Ballet who is known for her extraordinary discipline and work ethic. She also is now happily married to the artistic director of the company, Peter Martins, and has a lovely baby girl. One day a week, she teaches the children's and intermediate divisions at the School of American Ballet. As you can see, her life is well rounded, and she's gaining experience as a dance teacher, a real asset if she makes a career transition to teaching after retiring from the stage.

Another example of someone who's created a balanced life is Mikhail Baryshnikov, long considered to be one of the greatest male ballet dancers in the world. Friendships with a variety of people, from Liza Minelli to Isabella Rosselini; children; and a long-term relationship haven't hindered his dance career, which continues to evolve from ballet to his current explorations in modern dance.

---

Companionship, love, and family create a much-needed balance to dancers' lives. Still, there are no hard and fast rules about including people in your world; everyone's need for closeness is different. Just keep an open mind, and make sure that the personal sacrifices you make are necessary. In the next chapter, we take a closer look at some of the hard choices dancers have to face as they try to establish a professional career. To help you out, I take you through the steps of finding and keeping a job in dance. Résumés, photos, and networking are just some of the tools that you'll need to succeed.

# $\int$o You Want to Be a Professional

*M*ost dancers dream of performing on stage. Yet I know that jobs are getting harder to find as the technical level of dancers increases and rising costs, coupled with a lack of funding, force dance companies to cut back. Three out of four professional dancers currently get by on less than part-time employment, apprenticing for a small fee per ballet or doing industrials and toy fairs. Can anything increase your chances of success?

If you want to make it as a professional, you'll need a good "survival job" to cover your basic expenses as you look for work in dance. Next, it's important to fine-tune your audition materials so they show you at your best. The final step to a great dance job comes from using all the available resources to get good roles, a position in a dance company, or promotions. We begin this process by mapping out ways to help you survive.

## Survival Jobs

By the time many dancers tackle the problem of survival, they're often flat broke and in a state of panic. This often leads to acts of desperation. I've seen dancers leave New York City and go home because they couldn't pay their bills. Others make ends meet but take a big risk: They serve drinks in skimpy outfits, perform as exotic dancers, or give sensual massages. I know only one twenty-one-year-old unemployed performer who prepared to support herself while she was still a student by enrolling in a certificate program to be a trainer in the Pilates method—a conditioning program used by many dancers to build strength and flexibility. Most dancers end up waiting tables or working in bookstores, barely covering their rent even when it's split three ways. If any of this sounds familiar, it's time to take a look at your options. For you dance students, it's never too early to prepare.

## Make a Personal Inventory

Recently, I asked a group of dancers at the Alvin Ailey American Dance Center to suggest some interesting survival jobs. No one said anything. Instead, I got a roomful of blank stares, making me realize just how much dancers need help with this issue. The fact is that it's easy to forget about your other interests when you're trying to become a professional dancer. As you know, serious dancing takes time, energy, and a big commitment. Yet your interests, along with your abilities and personality, are the ingredients that create a match between you and another job. So take a moment to do a personal inventory.

Do you like to cook, read books, take care of animals, knit leg warmers, or do arts and crafts? Whatever your interests may be, pay attention because they're most likely to motivate you and lead to job satisfaction. This happened to a thirty-five-year-old musical theater dancer who loves to organize things, especially closets. It started as a joke when he offered to help out a hopelessly messy friend. Now, he's turned it into a lucrative part-time job. Another twenty-four-year-old ballet dancer is an amateur photographer. She translated this interest into a good survival job after realizing that many of her colleagues needed dance photos at a reasonable cost.

To match a survival job with an interest, you need to have ability in the same area. Some dancers develop their potential by training, using home-study programs, educational seminars, certificate programs, or college courses. If you decide to go to college, make sure that this doesn't conflict with your dance career. Of course, your parents may worry that putting off college is a bad idea. This was the case for Lauren, who wrote to me, asking for advice:

> My parents want me to go to college before I become a
> professional ballet dancer. Are there any ballerinas who
> have done this and still made it big?

I don't know of any ballerinas who've gone to college before getting into a big company. Typically, an artistic director hires you in your late teens, although experienced professionals often move on to other ballet companies at a later age. It's rare, however, for female dance majors in college to get a position in a ballet company other than one affiliated with their university. Your chances of getting an entry-level job in your twenties are higher if you're a talented male ballet dancer, simply because there are fewer men in dance. My advice is to focus first on ballet. If you get into a dance company, try to take one college course at a time in between tours.

Dancers who want to find a good survival job also need to take their personality into consideration. This may sound strange, yet certain characteristics affect job performance. For example, if you have a high need for achievement, how do you like to reach your goals? I know a jazz dancer who prefers to take a direct approach, relying on her own efforts to design dancewear. This differs from the style of a modern dancer who enjoys getting others to accomplish his goals as the director of a small dance group. Then, there's a ballroom dancer who loves teaching dance students. Why? Because she likes contributing to the accomplishments of others.

Whether you're extroverted or introverted on the job is also important. In general, extroverts are more sociable, cheerful, optimistic, active, and energetic compared to the reserved, submissive, even-paced personality of introverts. One musical theater dancer's outgoing demeanor made her a regular extra on a soap opera, where she made about $100 a day. In contrast, a more subdued ballet dancer excelled at tasks, and sewed toe shoes for money from one of the major shoe stores. She also loved animals and would "dog-sit" for company members who went on tour.

Finally, it helps to consider your need for power, as well as your emotional stability. Are you assertive and bossy or accommodating and easily led? If you like being the boss, you might be a lousy wait-ress but a great manager for a restaurant. Likewise, your emotional stability, sensitivity, or proneness to irritation will affect how you re-spond to work demands on a daily basis. If you're still feeling lost after completing your personal inventory, call the hotline of Career Tran-sition for Dancers, which provides free vocational counseling and training information over the phone (see the Resource Directory).

## Unique Problems for Women

So far, we've been discussing ways to create a good survival job for all dancers. Women, however, experience unique problems that make life much more difficult. According to the most recent cen-sus, three times as many female dancers get by on less than part-time work compared to males. They also earn between four and five thousand dollars less than men annually! It seems that a number of obstacles keep women from achieving their goals in dance. Check out the factors that stop them in their tracks:

- Financial pressures

- Lack of opportunities

- Pregnancy

- Limited support

- Insufficient time

- Family responsibilities

My research shows that only 22 percent of female dancers get a full-time dance position compared to 61 percent of the men. Female dancers are also less likely to achieve principal status as professionals. To increase your chances of survival, take care of your financial needs first before you audition. It also helps to consider family planning, so you aren't caught off-guard. A highly talented twenty-two-year-old modern dancer had dreams of performing in the Merce Cunningham Company—until she got pregnant. It took years before she could begin a home-study program to become a day-care worker. Dancing, however, was out of the question as a single mother.

## Picking the Right Job

Ideally, a good survival job covers all of your basic needs, including food, housing, and health insurance. A bonus occurs when it's interesting and leads to a career transition. Although it's unlikely that you'll get everything you want, careful planning can provide you with a more comfortable fit. In Chapter Two, I show you how the work habits needed to dance add up to improve your grades in school. They can also make you an outstanding, energetic, and highly disciplined employee, so don't panic! Here are some job options other than waiting on tables:

- Caterer

- Makeup artist

- Massage therapist

- Designer of dance wear

- Dance teacher

- Personal trainer

- Pilates trainer

- Paralegal

- Graphic designer

- Word processor

- Nutritional counselor

- Dance photographer

Remember, try to take your interests, abilities, and personality into consideration when you make your decision. Then, prepare! One problem that may continue to plague you if you work part-time or freelance is a lack of health insurance. Fortunately, there's a new organization called the Dance Professionals Associates, which offers low-cost premiums to dancers and their families (see the Resource Directory). Annual membership also provides discounts on valuable services such as travel arrangements, graphic design (résumés and other documents), income tax, and chiropractic care.

## The Audition Package

Now that we've covered your basic survival needs, it's time to switch our attention back to dancing. The first step toward landing a great dance job begins with your audition materials, which need to be in tip-top shape. What's the goal? To show you at your best!

Talent, technique, weight—all of these factors are uppermost in your mind when you take the leap from student to professional. A résumé, on the other hand, rarely gets top billing, even though it may be the first item to cross a director's desk before an important audition. Is it time to brush up on your written materials? It depends on how much you want to make a good first impression.

The sole purpose of an audition package (résumé, photos, and, sometimes, a video) is to advertise your skills as a dancer. Many items catch a director's eye: youth, a good dance school, scholarships, well-known references, and stage experience. Each company director also seems to favor a certain style, so be prepared to do it their way—whether it's Tharp or Balanchine! In contrast, dance competitions select dancers who are technically able to handle an intense program of daily classes and performances, whereas summer courses choose students at a suitable level for their age group. If you're confused about how to write your résumé, it's time to find out more about this aspect of the profession.

## Your Dance Résumé

The initial step in preparing a résumé is the hardest, according to Sherrie Hinkle, the education coordinator at the School of American Ballet (SAB). She finds that students often have trouble "thinking of themselves as somebody entering the workplace. My job is getting them to see their experiences as something to present to a potential employer." She helps School of American Ballet students put together a résumé and makes sure that they have photographs.

Dancers without this guidance have a much harder time, because switching gears and marketing yourself after years of being a "good student" is difficult. Typically, the dance world teaches us to be nice people who wait to be asked, whether it's demonstrating a step in class or performing a role in an annual workshop. Yet dance is like any other profession: Networking is the opposite of not working. In fact, I often advise ballet dancers to set up an audition tour over two weeks, including meeting with different artistic directors. It pays to be active and make connections.

So what should you put in your résumé? The first rule of thumb is to be selective. Darius Crenshaw, a 1996 May L. Wien award recipient for most promising male student at SAB, remembers that he used to go overboard and put everything down as performing experience. "I put the most important parts down but sometimes I also put down the ones that aren't so necessary." No director has time to wade through three cramped pages that end with a performance at age ten as *The Nutcracker* prince. Instead, try to limit your dance résumé to appropriate roles that fit within one neat, well-organized page.

## Where Should You Begin?

It's standard practice to start your résumé with basic information, including your name, address, phone number, date of birth (optional only for musical theater), weight, and height. Don't include hair and eye color unless you're like an eighteen-year-old dancer I know who wants to audition for musical theater. For dancers who aren't American, add your citizenship and work status (such as green card or visa). The rest of your résumé should cover performing and training experiences, which differ depending on your status: Experienced performers can focus more on featured roles, whereas students with limited stage work can use more space on training (such as Royal Academy of Dance, or RAD, certification). All dancers should include scholarships and awards.

Dancers who are looking for a job might also benefit from tailoring their résumé to a specific audition, as "Jerry" did, a talented modern dancer. His dream was to perform in the Martha Graham Dance Company, so he listed all the Graham pieces that he'd performed as a dance major in college. For job auditions, it also helps to include your own choreography in a résumé (if improvisation is required), drama roles (if a part calls for acting), or anything else that's impressive.

Finally, it's often useful to list the names, addresses, and phone numbers of three to four references at the end, if they're known to the director. Otherwise, mention them in your cover letter or put them on a separate page along with any highlights of newspaper reviews. Ask permission to use their names first, and keep them up-to-date.

## Choosing a Format

Though there's no one right way to put together a résumé, it must be neatly typed in a chronological or functional format.

The chronological résumé is the most widely accepted format because it gives a complete history of your dance experience, beginning with the most recent event in each category and working backward in time. Darius used this format, which focused on performances, schools, and dates rather than specific choreographers or roles. The sections include "Performing Experience" and "Training" (listing dance, drama, and singing for musicals). A good student résumé resembles the outline by Sherrie Hinkle for SAB shown in Exhibit 5.1.

The functional format differs from a chronological résumé in several important ways. Instead of including dates, you focus only on your strengths while bypassing your job history. The general sections include "Professional Activities" (or "Featured Roles") and "Training." I know a twenty-six-year-old modern dancer who used this format because she'd taken four years off to have a baby. Some dancers also use this format if they've started training at a later age. The danger is that a director could become suspicious, because your résumé lacks complete information.

It's also possible to write a résumé by employing a combination of both formats. In this case, you would use the chronological format with dates, while including some benefits of the functional format, such as mentioning well-known teachers in the education section or featured roles on stage. I know many musical theater dancers who also include a section on "Special Skills" near the bottom, such as second languages, playing an instrument, rollerblading, or horseback riding. Whatever format you choose, remember to present information that shows you at your best.

## Photos and Cover Letters

A dance résumé is without a doubt the centerpiece of your audition package. Still, your materials would be incomplete without photographs; you'll also need a cover letter if you're auditioning for a dance company by video or by taking company class. These elements comprise your best marketing tool to schedule an audition.

## The Cover Letter

Make sure that you address this to the *current* director. If you make the mistake of addressing your cover letter to the former director,

**Exhibit 5.1.  Résumé Outline.**

| | |
|---|---|
| Your Name _____ | Age _____ |
| Address _____ | Height _____ |
| City _____ | Weight _____ |
| Telephone _____ | |

*PERFORMING EXPERIENCE*

| | |
|---|---|
| School of American Ballet | Workshop Performances 1996, 1997 |
| | Principal roles in *Symphony in C, Serenade, La Ventana*; soloist roles in *Stars and Stripes, Who Cares?, Mozartiana*; corps roles in *Sleeping Beauty, Harlequinade.* |
| Next most recent/important | Stamford Nutcracker. |
| Earliest/least important | Description |

*OTHER WORK EXPERIENCE* (List first for survival work)

| | |
|---|---|
| John's Coffee Shop | Waitress, 9/94–present. |
| Orwell's Animal Farm | Pit bull trainer, 10/94–4/96. |
| Earliest experience | Description. |

*DANCE EDUCATION*

| | |
|---|---|
| School of American Ballet | 9/94–present: levels C-1-D. Teachers: Peter Martins, Suki Schorer, Tumkovsky, etc. |
| Dolly Dinkle Academy of Toe, Tap, and Baton | Dates, description, teachers. |
| Summer Courses | San Francisco Ballet 1996 |
| | Omaha Ballet 1995 |
| | Wagoner Ballet Theater 1994 |

*ACADEMIC EDUCATION*

| | |
|---|---|
| Harvard University | Ph.D., June 1997, Nuclear Physics. |
| Professional Children's School | High school diploma, June 1995. |

*REFERENCES*

List 3–4 people familiar with your work, including their addresses and telephone numbers.

*Source:* Courtesy of Sherrie Hinkle.

it'll end up in the trash. (A subscription to at least one dance magazine can keep you up to date on hirings and firings.) It's also important to type this letter neatly on the same brand of paper as your résumé, preferably heavy bond paper in a light color, using three-quarter-inch to one-inch margins. One sixteen-year-old ballet dancer who found typing to be beyond her capabilities used professional services listed in the weekly trade paper *Backstage*.

Begin your first paragraph by mentioning a mutual acquaintance or something special about the company, along with why you want to audition. Try to avoid the "cattle call" (open call) by asking to take company class if you can afford to travel. The director can see how you fit in with the other dancers, and you'll get a feel for the company and its home city. Be aware that directors aren't always crazy about this approach, so say that your schedule only allows you to audition on such and such a date (make sure the company's around). Then, include a letter of introduction from a trusted teacher who's known to the director, especially if it's a large company, like San Francisco Ballet.

The next two paragraphs of your cover letter should highlight your professional experience and summarize your dance training. In the conclusion, you can mention if a video is available; then, thank the director and say you'll call back in two weeks to arrange an audition.

Because directors judge dancers primarily on their body type and line, photographs are also crucial to your audition package. Include only *current* 5-by-7- or 8-by-10-inch black-and-white glossies (size depends on the requirements): a head shot with one or two full-body shots (a pose showing flexibility or a jump for strength) *sans* camouflage. Whether you're a man or a woman, it's best to wear simple practice clothes or a tight-fitting costume. If you can't afford a photographer through your dance school, ask if there are any amateur photographers in the affiliated company. I know one innovative eighteen-year-old who also used photos from a recent workshop performance. Order at least twenty prints so you can send them to different directors and still have enough left for the actual audition. Write your name on the back of the photos. Staple the head shot to the back of your résumé if you're in musical theater.

## Videotapes

The last piece of the puzzle for dancers is a video. Dance academies like the School of American Ballet require a video (but not a résumé) from foreign students who can't audition in person. Competitions, scholarship awards, and dance companies may also ask for a dance video.

Virginia Brooks, a professor in film production at Brooklyn College who does videography at SAB, suggests that you ask a friend with a camcorder and a tripod to tape you in a dance studio. Pick a simple background without a piano or mirror and wear a pastel leotard. If you wear a black or white leotard, the contrast between you and the background will make you appear heavier than you are. Make sure the light is adequate.

Keep the video short (under five minutes) and dance alone or, at most, with a partner with whom you've worked before. A good dance video often includes a short variation, excerpts from a live performance, or steps from dance class (such as an adagio, allegro, petit allegro, and pirouette combination). If it's for a competition or scholarship, find out whether there are specific requirements. Try to focus on your strengths, whether these are jumping, turning, or extensions.

Dr. Brooks says it's best if your friend starts with a close-up of your face as you introduce yourself. For example, "My name is Linda Hamilton. I've studied for eight years at the School of American Ballet. I'm auditioning for your company today. My audition tape will start with an adagio followed by an allegro, petit allegro, and pirouette combination." Or, "I'll be dancing the Lilac Fairy variation from Petipa's *Sleeping Beauty*, with music by Tchaikovsky." When you've finished, your friend should pull back (zoom out) and enlarge the frame to include your whole body with you standing naturally for a moment, and then stop the camera. Remember to look relaxed, and smile!

Next, mark out the steps so that your friend knows where to move the camera as you dance. If you move left, the camera should "pan" left, keeping you in the left side of the frame rather than in the center. You can also edit the tape yourself by having your friend stop taping after an exercise. Professional editing is costly and may remove the wrong parts—but never stop the camera in the middle of a variation! One sixteen-year-old dancer did this, giving viewers the impression that she either messed up the step or lacked stamina. When you're finished, hold the last pose for a couple of breaths, then cut. You'll look more confident if you seem to be having a good time.

To make the video look top-notch, check out the Yellow Pages for a professional video tape transfer that'll add titles and make copies (VHS is the best format). Don't forget to label your tape with your name, address, and phone number, plus the name of the piece, the date, and the choreographer if it's of a performance. Then, send your entire package (résumé, photos, and the rest) to the director about four weeks before you plan to audition. Remember to identify the contents as "Audition Materials."

### Make the Phone Call

Directors are busy people, so call the assistant or secretary about ten days after you've sent out your audition package. The best time to reach this person is often between nine and ten in the morning. State your name, ask whether they've received your audition materials, then tell them when you hope to schedule an audition. If this person can't help you, ask who can and when it's best to call back (remember to get the extension and phone number). Then, thank this person for taking the time. Be prepared to try several times. When you do speak to someone who can help you, they may try to direct you to the open-call audition. Explain that you're calling to see whether you could audition on another date (specify). If this date isn't possible, ask about the day before or after.

As you can see, a lot goes into making a good first impression in dance, from fine-tuning your résumé to following up with a courteous phone call. It's now time to move on to the next step—finding a great dance job. To get hired, you can't leave any stone unturned. Find out how to maximize your chances for employment.

# Getting a Great Dance Job

Way back when, many of my friends who didn't get into the New York City Ballet went to Europe to find a position. Today, regional dance troupes have sprouted up across the nation, along with more opportunities to perform in dinner theaters, national tours of musicals, commercials, music videos, and television specials. So why are most dancers out of work?

One problem is the economy. Budget cuts in American and European dance companies have taken their toll, resulting in shorter seasons, fewer performances, and, most importantly, a smaller number of full-time positions. Meanwhile, there's been an influx to the West of superb dancers from Eastern Bloc countries and the former Soviet Union. Because the supply of dancers exceeds the demand, you'll need to market yourself in a variety of ways, whether your goal is to get a good role, a company position, or a promotion. Let's see how.

## Pick a Professional Dance School

If you have your eye on a dance career, try to choose a professional school noted for a demanding technique. Ballet and modern dancers get a double bonus if their school or summer programs are also affiliated with a dance company. In this way, you'll become a familiar face when it's time to audition. Be aware, however, that some big dance schools won't accept you in the future if you turn them down. I know a highly talented sixteen-year-old student who got into trouble a year ago when her second choice for a summer program wanted an answer before she'd heard from the school of her dreams. She chose the lesser school and has regretted it ever since.

A professional school offers many benefits. Besides getting letters of recommendation from well-known dance teachers, you'll have an opportunity to perform in annual workshops that attract company directors. Ballet dancers need to be able to perform classical variations from the Romantic repertoire (such as *Sleeping Beauty*), as well as more contemporary movements used by today's choreographers. Modern dancers can also increase their competitive edge by taking ballet and attending workshops given by company directors or choreographers. Musical theater dancers will need training in singing, tap, jazz, and ballet. There are many excellent schools throughout the country, so choose one or several to meet your needs.

So far, I've made picking a professional school sound relatively easy, but I'm aware that geography and lack of money can present some formidable obstacles. Many of the letters I get through my column in *Dance Magazine* are from students who live in small towns with one or two nonprofessional dance schools. If you've reached the advanced level at one of these schools, get an honest evaluation from a teacher at a professional dance academy. This feedback will let you know whether you're technically ready to audition for a higher level.

## Go Where the Jobs Are

To get a job, you must go to auditions—a lot! This can be stressful, time consuming, and expensive, especially if you're on an audition tour in Europe. Please don't sabotage your efforts by auditioning injured; this sends a negative message to the director that you're weak, injury-prone, or tentative. Weight problems are also a liability on a job hunt, including being *too thin*. I know a talented musical theater dancer who makes a point of being physically fit before she auditions. She also has a great mental outlook (a subject I'll discuss at length in Chapter Six) and wears attractive dance clothes, leaving T-shirts, sweat pants, and cumbersome leg warmers at home. It's not surprising that she's performed steadily for the last five years.

Dancers who're ready to audition can find out about open calls from notices on the bulletin board in their schools or through monthly ads in *Dance Magazine*. An eighteen-year-old ballet dancer also orders *The Calendar of Audition Dates* that comes in December (see the Resource Directory), which lets her know of dates, times, and locations, as well as audition requirements for upcoming events. If your interest is in jazz, tap, or hip-hop, check out the weekly ads in *Backstage* (it also has some ads for modern and ballet). One successful thirty-three-year-old dancer picks up her copy every Thursday rather than subscribing.

As you can see, timing is important if you want a chance at the majority of shows and dance companies that hold yearly auditions. I know a nineteen-year-old ballet dancer who missed her chance because she didn't contact European dance companies by October for vacancies in the next season. Dancers who want to perform in Europe must be ready to audition between November and February. If you attend company class, you may also be required to attend a later open call as a formality. Make sure that you've got a contract before taking on this additional travel expense. In America, the height of the audition season for ballet begins in the early spring.

Perhaps, the most stressful part of an audition is knowing that you can be cut at any time. Because this is such an important (and scary) topic, I give you strategies to help you perform at your peak in the next chapter. For now, be aware that a formal ballet audition is like taking a dance class with eighty other dancers. At least part of this will be on *pointe*. In contrast, modern dancers do a short warm-up on the floor followed by excerpts from the company's repertoire. Musical theater auditions generally focus on choreography from a particular show, with the additional possibility of a simple ballet combination to check your technique.

It's best to do a thorough warm-up before an audition, and then head for the front of the studio where you'll be seen. If you're taking company class, remember to introduce yourself to the teacher, explaining that you're there to audition. Afterward, try to speak to the director. While this can be awkward, it's useful to know whether this person would consider you if a contract is available.

### Using Company Directories

Dancers who want to perform in professional companies must thoroughly research this subject. Besides targeting directors or choreographers that hold appeal, you should pick several dance companies whose style, level of technique, and repertoire match your abilities. A directory can help you find qualified people and an acceptable salary, but be prepared to start off on a small scale. One seventeen-year-old dancer apprenticed with the New York City Ballet for a year before getting a full-time position. Another teenager joined Boston Ballet II; she moved into the senior company two years later. I know other dancers who start with regional companies or travel to Europe to get a job.

One excellent resource is *The Dance Directory*, which provides vital information on more than two hundred European and American ballet companies that range from professional to nonprofessional (see the Resource Directory). You'll get a brief biography of the director, ballet mistress, or ballet master, a description of the company, and the name of the affiliated school, if any. This directory also tells you other facts that'll help you to choose. These include number of dancers, work permits, apprenticeships, guaranteed work weeks, salary, health insurance, live or taped music, tours, repertoire, audition requirements, and arrangement with a college or university.

Once you've gathered this information, it helps to see the company perform. I worked with a seventeen-year-old dancer who trained at the School of American Ballet and American Ballet Theatre's summer program. First, we made a list of small and large companies that performed the Balanchine technique, as well as the more classical repertoire that he preferred. Then, he saw each of the companies perform. Besides noting whether he liked the company's style, he asked himself "Do I have a similar body type and technique as these dancers?" If the answer was no, he would set his sights on the next dance company.

Another way to check out a company is to do what a twenty-one-year-old modern dancer did: She watched videos of different dance companies at a library for the performing arts. After targeting several companies that matched her body type and style of training, she then asked the librarian for *Stern's Performing Arts Directory*. This book provides general information (director, number of dancers, taped or live music, official school) plus contact information for a variety of dance companies, including modern, ballet, ethnic, jazz, tap, historical, liturgical, and mime.

You may also want to find out about a company's pension plan, the possibility of choreographing (if this is an interest), and its policy on helping dancers with a career transition in the event of an injury or retirement.

**Should You Have an Agent?**

Until now, we've concentrated on what you can do to increase your chances of success. For some dancers, this also includes finding an agent for leading roles (agents don't take commissions on corps and chorus).

If you're a gypsy in musical theater who can sing, dance, and act in supporting roles, an agent is a good idea because you don't have the security of a position in a dance company. Instead, you must audition over your entire career for shows that may last a week or (if you're lucky) several years. An agent evaluates your talent, and sends you out for suitable roles in industrials, commercials, and musicals. This person also arranges a time when you can be seen, letting you skip open calls that attract hundreds of dancers. It's rare to sign an exclusive contract with an agent unless you've landed several jobs or callbacks. This really isn't so bad: principal roles are scarce, and you hand over at least 10 percent of your salary if an agent finds you work.

Agents can't get you into a dance company. If this is your goal, don't bother with an agent unless you want to do outside gigs. Judith Fugate, a former ballerina with the New York City Ballet, worked with an agent who collected 15 percent of her salary for booking tours and guest appearances during her company's lay-off. She didn't sign an exclusive contract, however, because the work was sporadic. She says: "Agents wait for people to contact them about jobs." Instead, she believes in finding work herself, networking with heads of university dance departments, company directors, and theater managers. Offers may also come from people who see you at your dance studio.

If you think an agent could help you, the speediest way to get an appointment is through a friend who works with one. Of course, you can also try your luck by getting a publication (see the Resource Directory). *Ross Reports Television and Film* is a directory of casting directors and agents in New York and Los Angeles that's revised monthly. *Stern's Performing Arts Directory* has an annual listing of agents. Be prepared to sing or do a monologue (but not dance) for the audition.

### Applying for Competitions

It seems strange to think about entering a competition if you want to dance professionally. Yet unlike dance conventions that expose you only to excellent teachers, a dance competition may actually get you work. The competition judges include prominent dancers, choreographers, and directors, thus giving you valuable opportunities to network.

How important is it to win? Winning a big competition opens the door to the best dance companies in the world. Yet the chances of getting first or second prize are slim. An example was the Paris International Dance Competition in 1996. Over two hundred dancers from thirty-nine countries competed in this event; eight dancers and two duos received prizes or recognition. Yet, even when you don't win, you can still get a job offer. A sixteen-year-old American dancer who made it to the Paris finals was offered a position in a German dance company!

If you feel up to the plunge, the first step is to send away for an application (see the Resource Directory). Be aware that most competitions now have contemporary and classical rounds, requiring different styles of dance. You'll also need to pay close attention to entrance requirements that call for a dance video of variations or a pas de deux. Finally, dancers who're accepted should give themselves time to prepare mentally and physically to face stiff competition. Check out Chapter Six on how to curb performance anxiety, so you'll be the best you can be.

### Once You Get a Dance Job, Make It Count

You've gone to all the important auditions, looked the competition squarely in the face, and that magic moment has finally arrived—you have a job! Whether it's performing in a Broadway musical or with the Miami City Ballet, you've taken a big step in your career. Are you ready for the challenge?

Company life is a mixed blessing. On the positive side, you get to perform on stage as a professional, while becoming a part of a close-knit family. Even today, I have special memories of the New York City Ballet, taking company class, and sharing the dressing room with the other dancers. When I retired in 1988 after dancing my last performance of *Chaconne*, flowers and good wishes sent me on my way.

Yet, in spite of this camaraderie, a dance company isn't a democracy. Your life work is entirely in the director's hands. Of the dancers who apprentice for peanuts, only a few move on to an entry-level position in the corps. On rare occasions, an exceptional dancer may be promoted quickly to a soloist and, later, a principal position. The majority, however, who're ready, willing, and able to perform better roles, may be ignored. Seniority also doesn't guarantee status. A twenty-nine-year-old corps dancer told me of her despair when an apprentice almost half her age was taken into the company cast in a principal role. Another thirty-two-year-old soloist lost his best roles to a new male dancer who'd caught his director's eye.

The dancers' importance to the company is also reflected in their salaries. For example, corps dancers in the New York City Ballet make between $800 and $1,325 per week, depending on seniority. The minimum pay for a soloist is $1,550 weekly, whereas principals negotiate their salaries with management. This could be as much as $130,000 annually. At the top of the pyramid are internationally acclaimed stars. When these dancers guest in a national dance company, they may make as much as $9,000 per performance. But what does the average dancer make? According to the most recent census, it's a meager $22,000 a year.

When no roles are offered, you can feel like an orphan. So take advantage of every opportunity to shine! I know an enterprising nineteen-year-old dancer who always makes a point of going to the front of class, learning new parts quickly, and replacing other injured dancers. The ballet mistress is now rewarding her with roles usually reserved for more advanced corps members. I know another twenty-five-year-old dancer who's taking her career into her own hands. Instead of waiting to be cast in leading roles, she's arranging outside gigs through a dance agent. These will help you get noticed by other directors, who may offer you a job, as well as show your own director that you're more than capable of handling additional responsibilities. Another twenty-four-year-old dancer is auditioning for a smaller company, where she'll get more of an opportunity to perform. Whatever you decide to do, set a goal, then go for it!

## Should You Join a Union?

There are clear benefits to belonging to a union. The rules don't change from week to week, and management can't ask you to do something that's unfair, such as rehearse until midnight. You'll also have access to health insurance. As a member of the New York City

Ballet, I was required to join the American Guild of Musical Artists (AGMA), whereas dancers in American Ballet Theatre belong to a new association, Independent Artists of America. However, some dancers don't have this option.

Many dance companies are nonunion. One twenty-two-year-old dancer couldn't afford to go to a doctor because of her small salary with no health insurance from her company. Another twenty-five-year-old musical theater dancer hadn't accumulated enough work to qualify for membership at the Actors' Equity Association. This dilemma turned out to be a Catch-22: Because she wasn't an Equity member, she often had last dibs at auditions, making it more difficult to find work (this isn't a problem in ballet companies). Similarly, you must also qualify for membership in the Screen Actors Guild.

I know one desperate dancer who finally decided to perform on a cruise ship and ordered listings of producers from back issues of *Backstage*. Fortunately, this is a good first job for jazz and tap dancers, because the position doesn't require union membership. She got free room and board, saving money for her return to New York. Of course, you can do this only if you can sing, are able to perform several dance techniques, and have a great personality.

Along with helping you to find work, a union can also create a harmonious workplace. Here's a letter from a dancer who experienced major problems in a non-union company:

> *I recently joined a ballet company that has a good reputation. The problem is that the director treats the dancers (especially the newer ones) very harshly. During our rehearsals, all comments and criticisms are yelled out in a rude, demeaning way. It's as if her intention is to keep us insecure and paralyzed with fear. The dancers talk about it and support one another, but we still have to please her to get good roles. Dancers need to be treated like human beings by their bosses. How can I deal with this short of leaving?*

I hate hearing stories like this. Unfortunately, no law prohibits yelling in the workplace. So unless you've actually suffered some form of discrimination—based on sex, race, religion, creed, national origin, disability or, in some places, sexual orientation—your best bet is to join the American Guild of Musical Artists or another performing arts union (see the Resource Directory).

According to Alexander Dubé, AGMA's administrator for dance management, union members can file official grievances against artistic directors and remain anonymous. It's also possible to include protective language in your contract. This states that your employer can't subject you to insulting or humiliating language or abusive contact, whether it's from staff, choreographers, ballet masters, teachers, or directors, because it may lead to injuries. Company dancers who want to join AGMA only need to take a vote among themselves; a director has absolutely no say in this decision.

In this chapter, the important message for professional dancers is to *prepare* for life outside the studio. I see many dancers who simply burn out after years of waiting tables. Yet it's possible to take the time to find a good survival job, which may even lead to another career—a topic we get into at length in Chapter Eight. You can also go far by sprucing up your audition materials to make a positive first impression. Last but not least, you need to market yourself and make the most of the resources available to you. Now is that so hard to do?

———————

In the next chapter, we take a look behind the scenes at problems that interfere with optimal performance in auditions, as well as onstage. Just like other athletes, dancers perform better when they believe in their abilities. Yet inexperience, critical teachers, and perfectionism can all make dancing in front of others a frightening experience. Before you let insecurity beat you down, find out how to manage your fears with strategies that help elite athletes go for the gold.

# 6

# *P*erforming
# at Your Peak

*I*s it time to screw up your courage and try out for a special summer program? Or are you egging yourself on to perform in a show or company? Competition is a fact of life in dance, for professionals as well as for students. Yet I know talented dancers who freeze before an important audition, whereas others think nothing of whipping off thirty-two *fouettés* in front of four thousand people! Why does performing spook some of us and not others?

The answer depends on a number of factors, ranging from dancers' training and stage experiences to their frame of mind. In this chapter, I discuss the obstacles that keep you from peak performance, along with paradoxes such as perfectionism, which can distract you from your goals. We'll also examine how excess anxiety leads to stage fright, with lapses in physical control, attention, or behavior. Finally, I discuss strategies from sport psychology that help to create optimal performance.

## Sources of Performance Anxiety

A live performance is breathtaking because it unfolds before your very eyes. Neither you nor the audience know the final outcome, making it exciting—and precarious, if you fall down or miss a step.

Some dancers may feel a silent battle raging inside, as fear and inhibition mount. Will you rise to the occasion, wowing your audience? Or will all of your self-doubts come crashing down on your head?

Some dancers feel insecure on stage; others find auditioning equally difficult because of the added pressure of having to compete with little chance of success. A recent example is *Tharp!*—a show of Twyla Tharp's choreography that auditioned eight hundred dancers in five major American cities. Only eleven positions were available, making the odds of winning a spot in this dance ensemble one in seventy-one, or 1.4 percent! One nervous performer told me, "The whole rejection process can really beat a dancer down. At the end of the day, you wonder what you did wrong." Before any of this happens to you, let's take a look at the road blocks that stop peak performance.

### Poor Training Experience

Training plays a big role in how you dance. Still, there's a lot more to performing than just technique. You also need to *believe* in your abilities. Research shows that people with high self-esteem do better performing in front of others, whereas those who lack confidence may easily lose their nerve. Although many factors contribute to self-doubt, bad training is especially troublesome.

In Chapter Two, I discuss dangerous teaching practices that lead to injuries. Is it any wonder that these methods also affect your confidence? My survey results from almost one thousand dancers show that those who are verbally attacked by their teachers suffer from stage fright: They feel excessive fear, constant alarm, and physical signs of anxiety compared to dancers without critical teachers. A similar reaction occurs in dancers whose teachers pushed them when they were injured. In both cases, these teaching behaviors cause more than psychic distress. They actually stop you from achieving your goals as a professional. One out of five dancers who have abusive teachers also describes a problem with self-sabotage.

The following case shows how this training background can compromise your performance.

"Maggie" is an eighteen-year-old musical theater dancer who came see me in tears after being unemployed for six months. Although a scholarship dance student, she found herself avoiding auditions because, "I know I'm just going to get cut." In fact, the few times that Maggie forced herself to audition often ended in critical mistakes, due to her anxiety. Her problems began after an especially stressful summer dance program, when a guest teacher (who was a former ballerina) ridiculed her constantly for minor mishaps. To combat her fears, I encouraged Maggie to find a supportive teacher. I also taught her techniques to focus her attention and reduce stress. After three months, Maggie approached auditioning with renewed confidence.

Though it's never too late to address the emotional aftermath of poor training, the best remedy is prevention. Try to audit a dance class before signing up to be sure that it's safe from abusive teaching practices. If this tactic is impossible, ask dancers who attend the class how they like it. Remember, there are many excellent dance schools; don't settle until you find what you need. In the last section, I discuss ways to help you solve problems that keep you from achieving your goals.

### Inadequate Stage Experience

Besides negative teaching practices, another factor that can affect your confidence as a dancer is stage experience. The less professional experience you have, the more uncomfortable you may feel in the spotlight. My research shows that dance students report significantly more problems with stage fright than retired or current professional dancers. This fact was born out to me not too long ago when I received a phone call from a concerned mother whose fifteen-year-old daughter was panicking because of an upcoming dance recital. What was the problem? It was this dancer's first time performing "on toe" outside of dance class.

Stage experience, whether it's dancing in toe shoes or doing challenging roles, helps you to feel more comfortable as a performer. Still, don't expect all of your anxiety to disappear. Here's a letter from a dancer who worried that preperformance nerves were a sign of trouble:

> *My goal is to stop being anxious onstage. Every time I do a solo my heart pounds and I feel really nervous. Yet nothing bad ever happens and I eventually calm down. What's wrong with me?*

Absolutely nothing! It's normal to get nervous right before you perform, even if you're experienced. Just ask pilots, public speakers, students taking exams, or Olympic athletes. This reaction gets you ready for action, and usually diminishes several minutes after you start to dance. One leading male ballet dancer told me that his residual nervousness made him feel more focused, helping him to achieve a brilliant, hard-edged clarity. A normal case of the jitters can also increase your motivation by making you practice for a special event until you've nailed it.

In contrast to the good aspects of anxiety that lead to arousal and intensity, apprehension and distraction can cause problems for professional dancers who rate their fear of performing as "excessive." Again, stage experience seems to be an important factor. Corps dancers report significantly more fear than soloists or leading dancers, and are more likely to avoid performing in front of others.

What can you do? If you're a student, try to attend a dance school that offers opportunities to perform in annual workshops, recitals, and other productions. Dancers can also gain valuable experience through dance competitions and freelance work (see Chapter Five). Of course, this is easier said than done if you're afraid to take the first step. To move forward, check out the mental strategies in the last section of this chapter.

## Perfectionism

I receive letters all the time from dancers who will not be happy unless they're perfect. Up to a point, it helps to be a perfectionist in dance, or you'd never be willing to repeat the same steps over and over again. Yet it's easy to end up frustrated. I know hypercritical dancers who make no allowances for flaws regardless of anatomy, fatigue, age, or genes. If your goal is perfection, then you'll always fall short. After all, who's perfect? Being hypercritical may also hurt optimal performance. This letter came from a dancer who learned this lesson the hard way:

> *Maybe I'm being too hard on myself, but it seems like I'm my own worst enemy. If my performance isn't flawless, I lose my concentration and my dancing falls apart. It's getting to the point where I'm almost afraid to perform. Do you have any suggestions?*

Dancers who demand perfection can develop a negative self-concept and sabotage their best efforts. This is what happened to "Jeffrey," a twenty-three-year-old modern dancer in a national company, who came to see me because he felt like he was losing his career. On the surface, he was a serious, hard-working dancer who'd made remarkable gains in his technique over the last five years. Unfortunately, Jeffrey was terrified of making mistakes. To prepare for solo roles, he would take three classes a day, swim twenty laps, and do Pilates exercises. This approach resulted in a lackluster performance and, eventually, a serious injury. Together, we revised his schedule to reduce his fatigue. Jeffrey also learned cognitive strategies to quell the negative voices inside that told him mistakes were bad, strategies that helped him take greater risks on stage.

A perfectionist thinks, "If I'm not flawless, I must be horrible." Yet, if an athlete can win a gold medal without scoring a perfect ten, the same principle must hold true for dance. Instead of making a giant, illogical leap from the fact of a small mistake to the specter of a failed performance, take a realistic look at your abilities and chances of success. Perfection works best as an ideal—you can desire it, and the desire leads to a dynamite performance. Demanding perfection, however, can sabotage your career. Because cognitive distortions can impair performance, I discuss this topic in the section on stage fright.

## Competitive Feelings

Another personal habit that leads to insecurity in dance is constantly comparing yourself to others. This habit is often difficult to spot, because dancers learn by watching others. Still, competitive feelings may cause you to put your self-esteem on the line. It's like riding an emotional roller coaster. One day you're up, the next day you're down—all because of someone else's performance.

This is what happened to a twenty-four-year-old dancer from California who found herself focusing on size. She recalls, "You look at people who are taller, who have longer legs, longer extensions. You start to think, my legs aren't that long. My extension isn't that high." Yet comparisons can be deceiving. I know many good dancers who come in all sizes and shapes. Some look quite ordinary at the *barre* but they absolutely blossom in the center. Others make up for their weaknesses by capitalizing on their strengths.

The best performers convey a joy that transcends body parts or technique, taking their audience into another realm. Yet, as you've seen, a number of obstacles can get in the way. In the next section, we look at the price that dancers pay when the pressures around being watched become overwhelming. Serious problems, ranging from stage fright to efforts to self-medicate with alcohol and drugs, make performing a dangerous experience. Fortunately, it's possible to correct these problems by using many of the mental strategies outlined at the end of this chapter.

# Symptoms of Performance Anxiety

In contrast to the healthy amount of anxiety that increases arousal and intensity, stage fright gives you the willies. The fear is excessive and unrealistic. In a survey of 2212 members of the International Conference of Symphony and Opera musicians, 24 percent reported stage fright as a primary health complaint. What about dancers?

Until recently, most researchers bypassed dance in their efforts to understand performance anxiety, perhaps because dancers rarely complain. Yet when I conducted my *Dance Magazine* survey of 960 dancers, I found that 40 percent suffered from symptoms of performance anxiety. Some of these dancers' symptoms were physical, whereas others struggled with mental anxiety or problem behavior. Let's take a look at the various ways that stage fright can take hold of you.

## Mental Anxiety

What do you really think about yourself? You should know, because this has a direct effect on your feelings and behaviors. Positive, self-enhancing thoughts can improve your performance. In contrast, people who're riddled with negative "self-talk" undermine their confidence, making it less likely that they'll focus on the task at hand— a habit that often interferes with peak performance. See if any of these cognitive distortions, adapted from the late Dr. Eugene Gauron's work with athletes, ring true.

- You view things in black-and-white terms, using one-dimensional labels in dance, like *loser*.

- You expect the worst in every situation, whether real or imagined.

- Your self-worth depends entirely on your involvement or success in dance.

- You overestimate your responsibility for every mistake or failure as a dancer.

- You think it's always unfair if someone else's idea of what's best in dance goes against your wishes.

- You blame all your problems on external sources, such as teachers, theater conditions, directors.

- You predict the future based on a single incident that keeps you from making the most of opportunities.

Faulty beliefs underlie distorted thinking, yet they may have little to do with reality! I know a gifted twenty-one-year-old dancer who operates according to the belief that her talent can disappear at any time. If this dancer has trouble with her pirouettes, she panics, thinking, "I'll never be able to turn again." Then, she gives a 110 percent effort to correct the problem, even if it's due to fatigue or sore muscles. Yet the truth is that all dancers have off-days, and talent doesn't disappear in your twenties (unless you're disabled). If you're being excessively self-critical, stop—it's time to be objective. In the last section, we review various techniques to reduce mental anxiety.

**Physical Anxiety**

Imagine that you're watching a scary movie. Suddenly, you hear a piercing scream as a person jumps out of the darkness. Your heart is pounding. Your fists are clenched. The movie has just activated the "flight-or-fight" reflex designed by nature to help you flee or attack a hidden enemy. Most people like to be scared (a little), so this reaction is rarely a problem except with chronic stress, which ruins your health. Physical anxiety is also necessary for performing, because it adds intensity to your performance—but I know some nervous dancers who feel like they're about to lose their lunch during the opening strains of *Swan Lake*. Here's what it's like to have a bad case of physical anxiety.

You enter an audition or step on to the stage. Instead of getting caught up in the magic of the moment, your body reacts as though you're being attacked by a lion. The blood flows immediately to your large muscles to help you get away, resulting in a bad case of indigestion. Your muscles tense, forming a body "armor" and making your back ache. You become hypervigilant to small sounds and movements. A dancer with the Martha Graham Dance Company describes this kind of sensation as his body having a mind of its own. He says, "I get a stomachache and headache. I start twitching in my fingers, and I bite my nails."

You may also experience excessive sweating, a dry mouth, cold hands, tremors, or heart palpitations. Besides alarming you, physical symptoms of anxiety can disrupt the fine motor control needed to dance. The antidote to this problem ranges from soothing music to exercises that reduce muscle tension or promote a state of deep relaxation. I'll show you how to reduce physical anxiety later on, as well as ways to reframe your experience with mental skills training so that a rapid heart beat, for example, becomes a positive sign rather than a cause for alarm.

## Behavioral Signs of Stage Fright

Your fears also affect how you behave. Under the right circumstances, some dancers may find that nerves increase their motivation to practice for an upcoming event until they feel confident. Too much anxiety, however, can lead to behaviors that signal increasing tension, over and above the efforts to control the outcome of the performance. Though these actions may be harmless, others can actually interfere with your career.

For example, one twenty-two-year-old ballet dancer would become agitated and begin to pace right before a competition. As her tension increased, she responded by following a number of superstitious rituals, such as wearing her "lucky earrings," warming up in a particular sequence, and crossing herself three times before her performance. These behaviors served to reduce her anxiety, as long as she didn't lose an earring! Yet some dancers may also struggle against their own best interests. Let's see how.

I know dancers with stage fright who avoid auditions, hide out in the back of a studio, or overpractice until their muscles are crying out for relief. These actions reduce anxiety at the expense of their long-term goal to succeed. Remember, you do yourself a big disservice when you back away from auditions or refuse to network. Likewise, be careful if you face your fears by constantly pushing your body. A serious injury will cause all that hard work to go down the drain. If you think your actions are leading you down a dead end, it's time to reevaluate your approach. Later on, I will show you goal-setting strategies to help you stay headed in the right direction.

## Do You Have Stage Fright?

Now that you know about stage fright, take a moment to list any symptoms giving you trouble. Remember, it's normal for performers to get anxious, so only list problems that get in your way. A full-blown case of stage fright will either interfere with your performance or cause you intense anguish. Sometimes, it does both. The American Psychiatric Association describes this problem as a "Social Phobia," based on the following criteria:

*Diagnosing Social Phobia*

1. You show a marked and persistent fear of one or more social or performance situations, in which you're exposed to unfamiliar people or possible scrutiny. You're afraid that you'll do something to humiliate or embarrass yourself.

2. All it would take for you to experience intense anxiety or even a panic attack is to enter this situation.

3. You recognize that your fear of performing is excessive or unreasonable.

4. You avoid performing in front of others, or else endure it, suffering intense anxiety or distress.

5. Your avoidance, anxiety, or distress around performing interferes significantly with your daily routine, occupational functioning, or social relationships. Even if there's no disturbance, you're still extremely upset about having this phobia.

6. If you're under eighteen, these symptoms have lasted at least six months.

7. Your fear or avoidance isn't due to the physiological effects of substance abuse or a health condition. Your symptoms also aren't caused by another mental disorder involving panic, separation anxiety, a morbid preoccupation with a minor physical defect, pervasive developmental failures, or detachment from others.

8. If you have a general medical condition (such as stuttering) or another mental disorder, these have nothing to do with your social phobia.

Stage fright strikes at the heart of what you love to do best—dance! As a result, people who suffer from performance anxiety are twice as likely to become depressed and dependent on alcohol in an effort to self-medicate. They may also use recreational drugs to combat anxiety. Though wanting to feel better is understandable, self-medication causes more problems than it solves.

## Self-Medication: Making a Bad Situation Worse

Why would anxious dancers want to get high? Self-medication is alluring because it produces a pleasing state of euphoria, reduces the tell-tale signs of stress, or gives you an instant—and artificial—boost of energy. The problem is that it may also lead to mood swings, allergic reactions, or dependence—none of which enhance your performance on or off the stage. Though the initial danger signs are often subtle, the end results can be deadly.

One of the first signs of trouble is drug tolerance, which means that you must take increasingly larger doses to achieve the same effect. I know a thirty-four-year-old modern dancer who went from one drink to four every night to feel relaxed. With repeated use, you may also develop physical dependence, making it difficult to stop. Withdrawal symptoms run the gamut from anxiety, nausea, and severe stomach cramps to convulsions, delirium, and even death! Finally, all drugs, from LSD to alcohol, can cause a psychological dependence: You believe that you need the drug's positive effects to maintain your well-being.

Is substance abuse a big problem in dancers? I surveyed three hundred dancers and found that, as a group, things look pretty good. Although two out of three dancers (69 percent) drink alcohol by the time they're eighteen years or older, this is the same as the national average. They also drink moderately, averaging three drinks a week. The news about illicit drugs is even better: Dancers' drug use is five times lower than average compared to the general population (7 percent versus 37 percent). Yet look beneath the surface and you'll discover some problems.

In a survey of thirty-four professional dancers from a national company, I found that one out of four uses alcohol daily, because they're constantly under strain. Substance abuse is also higher among underage dancers in the larger survey ($N = 300$). Thirteen percent of dancers under eighteen years binge on alcohol, taking three to five drinks in a row. Weekly drug use is also higher in young female dancers, who use more barbiturates, designer drugs, amphetamines, and LSD (see Table 6.1). In contrast, the men's drug of choice is marijuana. Why are the male dancers in this study less likely to use drugs? Sometimes, wisdom comes with age. These dancers were more than fifteen years older than the females (average age forty, versus twenty-four for the women).

**Table 6.1. Dancers' Weekly Drug Use.**

| Type | All Dancers (percent) | | | Total (percent) | |
|---|---|---|---|---|---|
| | Age 18 and Under | Age 18–34 | Age 35 and Above | Male | Female |
| Marijuana | 29 | 90 | 100 | 100 | 65 |
| Barbiturates | 43 | 0 | 0 | 0 | 18 |
| Designer drugs | 14 | 9 | 0 | 0 | 12 |
| Amphetamines | 14 | 0 | 0 | 0 | 6 |
| LSD | 14 | 0 | 0 | 0 | 6 |
| Didn't specify | 14 | 9 | 0 | 0 | 12 |

Although many dancers experiment with drugs and alcohol without getting hooked, others become addicted or worse. For Alexander Godunov and Patrick Bissell, substance abuse was a death knell, cutting these former principal ballet dancers down in the prime of their lives. Remember, no one can control the ingredients in illicit drugs, and interactions between drugs and alcohol can be fatal. You also risk being charged with a misdemeanor for using illegal drugs and a felony for possessing large amounts that suggest an intent to sell.

Dancers who've developed a problem with alcohol and drugs need help. If you suspect that you fall into this category, the first step is to acknowledge it, because substance abuse is dangerous. Denial is a sign that something is wrong—it's not a solution! Happy endings for those who pretend there's no problem are rare.

Stage fright and substance abuse take a big toll—on your mind—as well as your body. The good news is that help is only a phone call away. If you need therapy, contact your local state psychological association or the International Association for Dance Medicine and Science (see the Resource Directory). Dancers who are physically addicted require a physician to manage the symptoms of withdrawal. Twelve-step programs such as Alcoholics Anonymous and Narcotics

Anonymous can also provide support for the psychological aspects of dependence. You don't need to handle these problems alone!

In the final section, we examine the strategies used by Olympic athletes to enhance performance. The pressures of performing are considerable, but the right approach can make a big difference in how you feel. Dancers who take control of their fears will also be less vulnerable to stage fright and related problems.

## How to Give Your Best Performance

Psychology has a number of techniques to enhance performance, such as goal setting, visualization, and anxiety management. The first step is to design a specific program that meets your unique needs. Whereas some dancers may require more stage experience, others need to reduce the physical and mental signs of stress. Next, make this program part of your dance routine, so you can *practice*. Finally, it's important to update your performance-enhancement program on a regular basis. Let's check out the following strategies.

### Goal Setting

So you want to be a better dancer but you're frustrated with your lack of progress. Setting goals will help you to focus your attention, increase your effort, and persist. You'll also feel less anxious and more confident, because you'll get feedback on a daily basis.

Unless winning and losing are the only goals that motivate you, it's best to stay away from any outcome goal that isn't under your control, like getting a specific job. Instead, choose a performance goal that requires a focus on self-improvement over a certain period of time. This goal must be attainable but challenging to help you reach your potential. Try to be specific ("I'll do five double pirouettes in a row by the end of the semester") rather than general ("I'll do my best to turn"). A nonperformance goal can also be useful ("I'll attend six major auditions in the next month"). Choose a couple of goals that have the highest priority, rather than overwhelming yourself with many.

Once you've chosen a long-term goal, it's important to break it down into several short-term goals that lead you in the right direction. I worked with a seventeen-year-old ballet dancer whose dream goal was to do thirty-two consecutive *fouettés* within four months. This amounted to eight extra turns a month and two turns a week. Her strategy involved practicing for twenty minutes after every class. She excitedly noted her daily progress in a small notebook, sharing the results with an understanding and supportive friend. Though it took her five months to hit her long-term goal, this represented a real achievement to this dancer.

Goals aren't set in stone. If you're lagging behind or ahead of schedule, make adjustments in your long-term goal. Getting periodic feedback from a teacher or friend also helps. Monitoring your progress and reevaluating goals over time can improve motivation and performance. You can't develop mental skills overnight, however, so try to be patient. Another psychological technique that can enhance performance involves using your imagination.

## Imagery Training

"Karen" is mentally preparing for her debut in a leading role in the New York State Theater at Lincoln Center. She imagines herself dancing confidently while leading the corps in her first successful performance. She *smells* the mix of perfume and sweat on her body as she waits in the wings. She *sees* herself run confidently onto center stage. She *feels* the power of her legs as she does her first explosive jump. She *hears* the orchestra playing as the audience applauds.

There are benefits to imagining yourself dancing a new role or doing a difficult step with ease. Besides creating a stronger belief in your abilities, research shows that imagery can improve your technique by giving you a mental blueprint to guide overt performance. In contrast, negative imagery is often detrimental to your performance. I know a talented twenty-five-year-old dancer who imagines making horrible mistakes before she goes on stage—and she has yet to get through a performance without a major blunder. It's helpful to turn adversity around with imagery (as a coping tool), but do this only occasionally and never before an important event. Instead, imagery works best when it's positive and self-enhancing.

As with all mental skills training, you'll be disappointed with imagery if you expect a quick fix. It only works if you make a commitment by practicing imagery skills regularly, similar to training your body. This involves three to four sessions a week, each lasting no longer than ten minutes. You can also use imagery daily by cuing into a particular sensory experience, word, or phrase. One twenty-three-year-old male dancer would imagine feeling his body burst with energy as he did big jumps in class. Here are the basic steps for using imagery to enhance performance, adapted from Dr. Rainer Martens's recommendations for sport imagery training programs.

1. *Sensory awareness.* Imagery is most effective when it's vivid. To heighten your sensory awareness, pay attention to what you see, hear, and feel (including your emotions) as you do a particular dance step. Then make note of sensations that cue you into the correct movement in a notebook. The more conscious you become of your senses while dancing, the more likely you'll be to recreate them through imagery. You can also practice imagining a recently executed skill while in class and rehearsal.

2. *Vividness.* After you've increased your sensory awareness through practice, it's time to develop and refine the vividness of your images by making them detailed, realistic, and clear. Find a dark, quiet place without distractions and relax (see next section for exercises). A simple way to practice imagery after you're relaxed is to imagine something small. I know one twenty-three-year-old jazz dancer who focused on the details of her leg warmers. As her imagery skills developed, she began to imagine more complex move-

ments associated with a specific jazz step. Be aware that the perspective is up to you. Some dancers prefer to imagine being inside their bodies, enhancing kinesthetic awareness. Other dancers like watching themselves in a movie, learning new skills and raising self-confidence.

3. *Controllability.* The last step in a training program is learning to manipulate and control your images. I know an eighteen-year-old dancer who was cast in a solo requiring a long series of *chaînés* (small half-turns on each foot traveling in a circle or in a straight line). Though her goal was to perform these turns beautifully, she began her imagery with a single turn, gradually working up to the whole series as she gained more control. Remember to modify negative images immediately by editing the material until you get a positive image. You can also slow down a movement to analyze your technique, or speed it up if your mind starts to wander, but the bulk of imagery should be in real time.

It's important to set goals in imagery using the previously described goal-setting strategies. Specify whether the goal involves technique, psychological skills, or overall artistic performance. Then, break down your dream goal into short-term goals, constructing a ladder. Repeat the imagery at each rung of the ladder until you get it right, in reality and in your mind, before moving on to more complex skills. It also helps to specify the actual scene, from practicing alone in a particular studio to working with your director and dancing the actual performance. If the floor is slippery, recreate this image and show how you'll cope with it. Once you get the hang of imagery, it can help you to

- Increase self-awareness

- Enhance motivation

- Focus attention

- Build self-confidence

- Reduce anxiety

- Acquire skills

Apart from regular ten-minute practice sessions, it helps to simulate movements in your imagery to increase kinesthetic sensation. I know a twenty-five-year-old ballerina who takes five seconds to simulate a correct movement along with the proper image after every mistake in class. After a successful performance onstage, she takes a few moments to reinforce what she did correctly. This dancer also keeps a notebook monitoring her daily progress and listing words, phrases, or feelings that trigger appropriate images. Finally, she uses the week before performing an important role to prepare mentally.

Imagery won't make up for poor physical skills or technique, but it can help you to reach your potential if you work within your real ability and cope successfully with new demands. You can also use imagery to improve your mood, focus, and motivation. If you don't see benefits after six to eight weeks, a psychologist who specializes in performance enhancement may be able to help you out.

## Cognitive Anxiety Management

Problematic thinking can interfere with peak performance. Although some dancers may believe that they perform best with no conscious thought, expecting all thinking to be shut off is probably unrealistic. Instead, you can use psychological techniques to change your thought processes and improve your performance.

In the preceding section on stage fright, I discuss a number of cognitive distortions that can get in your way. Certain general beliefs are problematic for people who become overly invested in their work. Some dancers may believe in the "no pain, no gain" principle or "practice makes perfect." One belief that I struggle with even now is thinking that I have to give 110 percent all the time. If you have doubts about whether a belief is irrational or ineffective, ask yourself whether you're being realistic. If not, nine times out of ten, you've probably latched onto an idea that isn't helping you to reach your goals, reduce conflicts, or decrease interpersonal stress. Dancers with faulty beliefs may be sabotaging their best efforts. Fortunately, research shows that cognitive restructuring techniques improve performance even more than other interventions.

## Self-Talk

Research shows that negative self-talk is associated with self-doubt and losing in sports, whereas successful Olympic athletes use positive self-instruction. The key to improving performance is gaining cognitive control. I know a twenty-two-year-old ballet dancer who was in the habit of raising her shoulders when she did large jumps. To change her technique, she instructed herself by using self-talk to describe the entire movement. You can also use self-talk to focus your attention in the moment ("Be here now"), to rev up ("Go") or relax ("Easy"), and to increase self-confidence ("You can do it").

Cognitive techniques help you adjust to a variety of external factors that heighten anxiety, such as the level of competition, the routine, or the setting. One nineteen-year-old dancer's fears increased after she moved up to a higher level of competition as a ballerina. She also felt insecure dancing with a partner versus performing on her own. Mental-skills training helped her out with these problems. How you look at factors outside of your control can also affect your performance, including the site (a large versus a small theater), touring in another country, or performing on an unfamiliar stage. The audience's response (friendly or hostile) and the presence or absence of friends and family are also important.

Other than becoming familiar with a new stage or asking your teacher not to see you in your first performance, you often have little control over external factors. You can control how you react to them, however, and to your own behavior. I often ask dancers to keep a daily record of their verbalizations during dancing, because it's the best way to identify the triggers and consequences of self-defeating thoughts. My approach is based on "Cognitive Strategies in Sport and Exercise Psychology" by Dr. Jean Williams and Dr. Thad Leffingwell. This log should include the situation where the self-talk occurred ("In the studio before doing a difficult step"), the content of the verbalizations ("I'll never make it"), and the consequences on your performance ("I missed the step") or your emotions ("Panic"), or both. It's also useful to record positive self-talk that facilitates performance.

The next step is to modify self-defeating thoughts by thought stopping ("Stop") and changing negative statements to positive statements ("I'm such a scared wimp in auditions" to "It's normal to be nervous in auditions"). To help you believe what you're saying, dispute self-defeating thoughts using facts, reason, and logic ("My heart's racing, I'm a wimp" to "My heart's racing, but this happens to all performers. It means I'm getting up for the audition. I've gotten through this situation before and I can do it now"). You can also reframe self-talk ("I feel like a nervous wreck" to "I feel excited and ready to go"). Behavior change is more likely to occur if you modify the belief underlying self-talk by using a combination of these techniques.

Besides enhancing performance, cognitive strategies can add to your self-esteem, personal growth, and development in all areas of life. Yet thought patterns often resist change, so you need to practice your mental skills daily.

### Regulating Physiological Arousal

No matter how talented or motivated you are, you need to be energized to perform at your peak. Whereas some dancers may need to get "up" for a performance or an audition, I find many more who want to reduce physical signs of anxiety. Exercises can help you to achieve your optimal level of arousal whether the problem is over-intensity or underintensity.

How much zip do you need? It depends on the activity. In weight lifting (a simple sport), athletes need a high level of intensity to exhibit strength and power. Dancing, on the other hand, is fairly complex, requiring focus, decision making, and fine motor control. This activity works best with moderate levels of intensity, although differences exist from person to person. For example, someone with an anxious personality (trait anxiety) may need to calm down more than a dancer who gets nervous in performance (state anxiety). Your health, fatigue, physical conditioning, and injuries will also affect the level of intensity.

Dancers who struggle with symptoms of overintensity may experience a range of reactions in response to the pressures of performance. The most extreme symptoms include tremors, muscle tension, breathing problems, and excessive sweating. Other, more subtle, signs may show up as fatigue, stomach butterflies, or a decrease in muscle coordination. I know an eighteen-year-old male dancer who would trip over his own feet during an audition, as his intensity escalated. He would also feel exhausted at the end of the day.

Though underintensity is less common, this problem can manifest itself in performers who're overconfident. Symptoms include reduced levels of adrenaline, heart rate, and breathing, leading to a lackluster performance or feelings of lethargy. You may spend less time warming up for an audition, or fail to review steps for a familiar role. A twenty-five-year-old veteran of musical theater said that she couldn't get motivated at an open call for a small show. It felt like she was "somewhere else." Fatigue from overwork, disinterest in performing, nutritional deficiencies, injuries, and sleep problems will also deplete the physiological resources needed to perform.

To decide how much intensity is best for you, Dr. Jim Taylor, a psychologist experienced in performance enhancement, and his coauthor of *Psychology of Dance*, Ceci Taylor, suggest that you take the following approach. First, see how your body reacts prior to and during a successful performance, so you can replicate it with specific exercises. This approach works well when combined with cognitive skills where you notice your thoughts and feelings at the time, as well as social influences, such as the presence of family and friends.

For example, you may notice that your best performance occurred when you felt physically calm and at ease. Your thoughts were positive, and your mother was present. Once you become aware of your body, thoughts, feelings, and the people around you, you're in a better position to work with the current situation. Repeat the same exercise, paying attention to your worst performance.

The second step is to regulate your intensity to its optimal level. For example, I know a twenty-six-year-old soloist who occasionally replaces injured dancers in smaller roles. To combat symptoms of underintensity, he uses high energy self-talk ("Let's go") and music to raise physiological intensity as he walks to the theater. He also makes sure to do a vigorous workout and use energetic body language by giving high fives to his colleagues.

Overintensity demands a different approach. If you're like many dancers who experience stress at the moment of performing, you take short, choppy breaths, leading to an inadequate supply of oxygen. This causes fatigue, muscle tension, and a loss of coordination—all of which can hurt your performance. It's easy to focus on these symptoms and become alarmed. Fortunately, you can often take the edge off by taking a few slow, deep, rhythmic breaths. By putting the focus on your breathing and reducing physical arousal, you also increase your self-confidence.

A more taxing problem associated with overintensity is extreme muscle tension, making you feel like you're made of stone. Besides inhibiting fine motor coordination, this problem can set you up for an injury. Progressive muscle relaxation is a useful way to get rid of body armor during a cool-down period or when you're trying to fall asleep, but it isn't appropriate immediately prior to dancing because you'll be too relaxed.

To achieve deep relaxation, you must first tense your muscles and then relax them. To begin, tense the muscles in your back and chest for five seconds as hard as you can. Then relax. Take a slow, deep breath. Feel the difference between the tension and the relaxation as you exhale. Repeat. Do the same exercise twice with your legs and buttocks, arms and shoulders, face and neck, and entire body. Each time you tense your muscles for five measured seconds, relax, take a deep breath, and feel the difference between the tension and relaxation.

The last exercise prescribed in *Psychology of Dance* to rid yourself of tension, anger, and frustration is smiling! Why? There are several reasons. According to research, people associate smiling with feeling happy and good. Smiling also alters blood flow in the brain, releasing neurochemicals that relax you. Finally, it's hard to hold onto negative thoughts and feelings when your body is expressing positive ones. Hold the smile for sixty seconds and feel your tension dissipate.

## A State of Flow

Everything's going right. In fact, you may even have moments when you're on cloud nine, existing in a place without fear, anxiety, or inhibition. This is what happened to the next dancer, who met a challenge without becoming overly anxious:

> *Something wonderful happened to me recently. I was*
> *rehearsing with this choreographer I really admire. The*
> *steps were difficult but everything was going very well.*
> *At one point, I suddenly felt this incredible rush of feeling.*
> *It was almost like I was entering another realm. What*
> *happened?*

Congratulations! When this happens, you've entered a state of flow: You're both concentrating and relaxed, even though you're facing a rather awesome technical feat. During these times, your mind begins to float in an effortless, unselfconscious way that's accompanied by feelings of ecstasy, harmony, and oneness with the universe. Dancers may even feel a strong spiritual component in their work.

Remember, if you want to achieve peak performance, you must consider your mind as well as your body. Positive change comes with awareness, control, and repetition. This is often difficult for dancers who face certain obstacles, develop stage fright, or attempt to self-medicate with alcohol and drugs. Fortunately, psychological interventions can help. Develop a program of goal-setting strategies, imagery, cognitive skills, or relaxation exercises that works for you and update it regularly. With consistent practice, these psychological skills will become automatic, requiring less time and effort to maintain the many lasting benefits.

---

In the next chapter, we examine dancers' physical health and well-being. Compared to the general population, dancers are more active, thinner, and less likely to smoke cigarettes or use illicit drugs. Still, injuries are a constant hex for dancers. Other health risks, like depression and eating disorders, are also higher than average, leaving dancers without health insurance at a distinct disadvantage. We'll confront these issues together, with an eye toward effective treatment and interventions.

# 7

# The Mind-Body Connection

*Injuries and Your Health*

*D*ancers are some of the fittest people around—when they aren't injured! Unfortunately, musculoskeletal problems come with the territory: 56 percent of leading dancers in New York City Ballet and American Ballet Theatre have a history of dance injuries, averaging ten months of disability during their career. Aside from musculoskeletal injuries, common health problems such as asthma can also compromise the close relationship between mind and body. Dancers ask me, "Am I accident-prone? Or are my physical problems due to poor habits, an underlying weakness, or inadequate training?"

In this chapter, we explore dancers' physical problems, beginning with injuries that arise from different factors. Treatment and prevention of dance injuries make up the next section. Besides working with your body, you'll need to cope with the emotional costs of injuries if you want to navigate the various stages of recovery. We conclude by discussing strategies to deal with common health disorders that make dancing an uphill battle. I'll also tell you about quality care and health insurance at a reasonable cost.

## How Common Are Dance Injuries?

The answer depends on whom you ask. For example, among students at the School of American Ballet, dancers with fewer anatomical

147

deficits are less likely to suffer a major injury than students less suited to ballet's requirements. It also helps to be flexible, but not hypermobile ("double-jointed"), if you want to avoid injuries. I know a beautiful sixteen-year-old dancer who's so loose and hyper-extended that she often has trouble controlling her body. A year ago, she underwent surgery to repair a torn knee ligament after falling in class. She's now using weight training on a regular basis to build strength. Research shows that hypermobility is an asset in the selection process in ballet but it's a liability in terms of injury prevention and sustaining a long career.

The risk of becoming injured also increases for dancers who become professionals. Why? Because you're dealing with a demanding schedule of tours, rehearsals, and performances, you're doing challenging choreography, and you're replacing other injured dancers at a moment's notice. To see what I mean, check out Table 7.1, which shows the injury patterns of almost a thousand dancers from my *Dance Magazine* survey ($N = 960$).

As you can see, professionals (active and retired) have significantly more injuries to the back, foot, hip, and shoulder than older or younger dance students. Chronic injuries that won't heal or will

**Table 7.1. Percentage of Dancers Reporting Injuries.**

| Dancers | Chronic | Arthritis | Back | Foot | Hip | Shoulder |
|---|---|---|---|---|---|---|
| *Students* | | | | | | |
| Over age 25 | 46 | 17 | 18 | 20 | 13 | 9 |
| Age 24 and under | 47 | 9 | 16 | 24 | 18 | 4 |
| *Professionals* | | | | | | |
| Active | 61 | 22 | 44 | 30 | 26 | 13 |
| Retired | 66 | 30 | 36 | 34 | 25 | 19 |

*Note:* All group comparisons are significant at .05, meaning that the likelihood of their occurring by chance is less than 5 out of 100.

come back and degenerative arthritis are also higher in professional dancers, peaking in those who retire. Can we pinpoint any one problem that sets you up for a fall? Not really. Typically, a cluster of factors leads to dance injuries. The good news is that serious, career-ending injuries are rare in dancing. In addition, by understanding the causes of injuries, you'll be in a better position to prevent them. Let's see how.

## Environmental Factors

Certain factors that lead to dance injuries may not be under your control. Sadly, dancers are often at the mercy of slippery or sticky floors, crowded studios, drafty theaters, heavy costumes, scenery, and stage effects. I remember slipping backstage in my fairy costume on the foggy residue in *A Midsummer Night's Dream*. It took six weeks, much of it spent in an air splint, before I could dance. Without even stepping onto the stage, I'd managed to partially tear my ankle ligament, resulting in a grade II ankle sprain with some joint instability.

Dance floors that are too hard or too bouncy are also a dancer's worst nightmare because bare feet, ballet slippers, and *pointe* shoes provide little, if any, shock absorption. Although there's one newly developed toe shoe that supposedly has high-tech, shock-absorbing cushions, most dancers continue to use *pointe* shoes made from nineteenth-century materials like burlap, cardboard, paper, and glue. Large dance companies, such as the American Ballet Theatre (ABT), reduce the number of impact injuries by constructing special suspended dance floors and bringing a portable floor on tour. This remedy is often too costly for smaller dance companies.

Environmental factors can also cause corns, blisters, and bruised toe nails. As a result, dancers often ask me for practical advice about treating sore feet, especially in toe shoes. A frustrated nineteen-year-old dancer told me that she's tried everything from special orders to a hammer to make her *pointe* shoes "fit like a glove." Yet she says that they still hurt and looked clunky. Obviously, there's a lot to know about this essential piece of equipment. Here are some basic tips.

Approximately one out of three dancers has bunions due to genes (not due to dancing). There's nothing we can do about genetics. You can slow down the problem, however, by not rolling in or winging your feet. Dance medicine specialists also say that wearing tight toe shoes will hurt you. To ease the pressure, *pointe* shoes must be wide enough to accommodate your bunions plus spacers or lamb's wool between your first and second toes. A toe shoe should also have a hard tip to prevent bruised toenails. Many dancers use Fabulon, a shellac sold at hardware stores, to keep the tip hard for longer use. In contrast, the shank (stiff insole) should be flexible. Try to break it in carefully so your ankle has both mobility and support. Generally, a higher vamp (top of forefoot) is safer for a flexible, high-arched foot, whereas a lower vamp gives stiffer feet more mobility.

Toe shoes come in normal, medium, or hard shanks. Many professional dancers also have special orders to fit their feet. Although fiddling with your shoes can get costly, dance shoe inserts are available in stores and catalogues (see the Resource Directory). Some toe-shoe makers will also make certain adjustments for free, as they did for a fifteen-year-old student who needed an extra-narrow heel to keep her shoes from falling off her feet. You'll also need to adjust the size of your toe shoes as your feet widen and lengthen with age. The shoes must be long enough to keep the toes from "knuckling" (curling).

After you find the best *pointe* shoe, the next step is to attach it securely to your foot. Dancers often sew elastic bands at the heel of a shoe along with ribbons on the side to keep it from slipping off. Tying the ribbons too tight, however, can be a problem. You need to rely on strong feet—not extra-tight ribbons—for support. I got a letter from two students in Nevada, asking me whether elastics damage the Achilles tendon. The answer is no. In fact, orthopedists advise dancers with tendinitis to sew elastics into their ribbons to remove the pressure on the tendons.

Many dancers also want to know how they can prevent blisters. Besides developing calluses and using tape, it helps to protect your toes in *pointe* shoes with gel-filled pads, lamb's wool, or paper towels. Other foot problems, like corns, often require a visit to the podiatrist.

Once a blister occurs, paint your skin with products like tincture of benzoin or Tuff-Skin to protect the skin under the tape. Always test these products first to make sure you aren't allergic. If you have open blisters, be sure to keep them clean, and apply an antibiotic first-aid cream to prevent infection. I know a twenty-six-year-old dancer who also uses an oral anesthetic intended for sore gums to deaden the pain from a blister. To keep the tape in place, even if you sweat, make sure that it's narrow (one-quarter inch) adhesive tape or moleskin. A modern dancer also told me about Elastikon made by Johnson & Johnson, which is a stretchable, porous cloth tape that molds to your feet. Even if you shower in it, it lasts for hours! For the best results, stretch it slightly over the curves of your feet or toes as you put it in place, avoiding any wrinkles in the tape that can irritate the skin.

Obviously, it pays to be careful about the potential hazards in your environment. Some problems are out of your control. Fortunately, there's a lot you can do to help your feet. At the end of the day, indulge yourself. A twenty-four-year-old dancer in musical theater soaks his feet in a tablespoon of Epsom salts and a quart of warm water. You can also use a lanolin-based lotion or "bag balm" to soften the soles of the feet to prevent skin cracks.

## Musculoskeletal System

Injuries also occur because of your anatomy. Each dancer is born with different anatomical strengths and weaknesses. For example, some dancers are highly flexible, and others are tight. Some have good natural turnout; others have poor turnout. Muscle mass also varies according to your genetic makeup. A seventeen-year-old dancer asked me: "How can I get rid of my big butt?" Unless you're taking anabolic steroids to increase muscle mass (please say no), there's nothing you can do about naturally big thighs or calves other than to work correctly and stay away from heavy weights.

Though the quality of your turnout depends on your natural ability, early training can improve it, though not dramatically. A young child who's pigeon-toed will almost never gain enough turnout to become a serious ballet dancer. In this case, it's best to focus on modern dance or jazz, where turnout is less important. This brings me to the subject of matching your technique to your body's natural abilities. One of the major causes of dance injuries is forcing your body to perform in an unsuitable technique, such as trying to dance ballet with poor turnout. Besides preventing unnecessary injuries, picking a technique that suits your body will make you more likely to succeed in dance. Then, make sure you work symmetrically by checking your placement in the mirror. Favoring one side predisposes you to overload injuries.

Anatomical limitations also exist for the older beginner in dance. You can only influence the skeleton while it's growing. Females reach physical maturity around age thirteen or fourteen unless there's a delay in menarche; males mature about two years later. The ability to mold your skeleton decreases dramatically after puberty. At this point, you can't really change your arches or turnout.

What can you change? You *can* improve strength, balance, timing, coordination, flexibility, and technique. You can make some of these changes on your own. Still, it's best to pay a few visits to a physical therapist who's familiar with dancers to help you develop a program based on your body's unique needs. If there's a major anatomical problem, you may need to be in a rehabilitation program supervised by a dance medicine specialist.

Though all dancers don't end up with serious aches and pains because of their work, the best way to prevent dance injuries is to make sure that your body is suited to your technique. Further on, I talk at length about warm-up and stretching exercises to reduce injuries.

### Steps, Style, and Technique

In Chapter One, I discuss how dance techniques differ in terms of training and style. With constant repetition, they also lead to unique stresses on the body. For example, classes in ballet and modern dance help to develop the flexibility necessary for executing the steps, but my *Dance Magazine* survey shows that dancers who study these techniques have significantly more arthritis (worn-down joints) than jazz or ballroom dancers. Males, who must partner and lift, also have more shoulder injuries. I know a seventeen-year-old male dancer who strained his shoulder after doing an off-balance lift in adagio class. Fortunately, a solid technique can offset these problems to some degree.

The timing of your dance training also has a big impact on your body, as you've seen. Be aware that it takes several years for the bones in your feet to hypertrophy (toughen), which protects you from impact injuries. You also need time to develop functional strength. Students who get a late start in dance or suddenly increase the amount of training must work carefully to avoid stress fractures. Early toe work can also be risky. Female dancers who begin *pointe* work before the age of twelve have more hip problems and tendinitis than dancers with more technique who start toe after this age. Still, a thirteen-year-old dance student with two years of training wrote to my advice column: "Why can't I go up on *pointe* now?"

There's no "right" age to begin toe work, although some Russian doctors believe that dancers who start at fourteen will have fewer injuries. The overall consensus is that it takes four years of serious training to develop the proper strength, timing, technique, and balance. At the School of American Ballet, children who begin ballet at age eight go on *pointe* in January—four years later! Toe work is given for fifteen minutes, three times a week, at the end of class. In the fifth year, students get to dance on toe for one full hour each week. While there's no evidence that early *pointe* work damages the bones in the foot, all dancers are vulnerable to certain injuries. For more information about the foot's anatomy and injury prevention, consult *The Pointe Book* (see Further Reading).

Certain dance styles can also take a toll on your body. According to Dr. William Hamilton, the consulting orthopedic surgeon to a number of ballet companies, injury patterns vary according to the type of choreography danced by the company. Dancers in the New York City Ballet, for example, are prone to different patterns of injuries than dancers in American Ballet Theatre. Juggling different techniques is also problematic for dancers who must adapt to today's choreography in "fusion dance." I know a twenty-eight-year-old ballerina who became disabled for three months after performing ballet and modern movements throughout an entire season. Like other professional ballet dancers, company class (in ballet) didn't train her for mixed repertoire. I encouraged this dancer to prepare her body for her next season by taking class in both techniques. She's now managing to perform fusion dance without any significant injuries.

To prevent injuries, make sure that your dance training gives you a solid technique. You need all of the following:

1. *Flexibility* to do the technique with the proper line
2. *Placement* to help you to move correctly from one step to the next
3. *Strength* to execute the steps, lift, and partner
4. *Stamina* to keep going in a demanding role or class

If you're having problems with your technique, consider doing a Pilates-based training program two to three times a week (see the Resource Directory). This method increases strength and flexibility, corrects muscle imbalances, and prevents injuries. Dancers who need to increase their endurance can also perform a low-impact aerobic exercise, such as swimming.

### Dietary Problems

Your eating habits also play a role in dance injuries, because dieting, low calcium intake, and weight fluctuations all interfere with bone density. If you stop menstruating, this problem gets worse: calcium leaves your bones in a manner similar to going through menopause, putting you at risk for stress fractures and osteoporosis. I know a fifty-year-old former ballerina who's getting ready for her second hip replacement, after thirty-four years of being anorexic. She has osteoporosis, and the first hip replacement didn't take.

You can also trigger muscle spasms with inadequate food intake, as well as from vomiting or abusing laxatives and diuretics. If you need to lose weight, do it the right way. You'll get better results and have fewer physical problems.

In Chapter Three, I describe the importance of sound nutrition and healthy weight loss practices. To lose weight safely, keep your intake around 1400–1600 calories a day with 25 grams of fat. An exception is if you're going through a growth spurt. Dancers who retain excess water may choose a low-sodium diet (1000–1500 mg daily). It also helps to drink eight glasses of water a day; otherwise, the body will conserve all the water it has. I know a twenty-three-year-old jazz dancer who became dehydrated because she incorrectly thought that drinking water makes you retain it. Chronic dehydration, on the other hand, causes a lot of problems, including kidney stones. Also, sports drinks should be consumed in moderation, if at all; they often contain a lot of sugar and can be constipating.

Dancers often ask me about sugar. Sugar should make up about 10 percent of daily calories. You don't have to cut it out completely. In fact, dancers usually rebel if they can't have a chocolate chip cookie once in a while. Some dancers also like to have tea with honey to give them energy before a performance. Finally, a healthy diet should include enough calcium to protect your bones. Female dancers need to take in 1500 mg of calcium daily from many sources, including dairy products, leafy green vegetables, or supplements. Male dancers need 1000 mg of calcium daily.

## Psychological Pressures

Considering the close tie between mind and body, is it any surprise that psychological pressures also contribute to injuries? My research on leading dancers in the New York City Ballet and American Ballet Theatre shows that those who are "overachievers" have significantly more injuries than their colleagues. Typically, enterprising dancers also make the mistake of coming back from an injury too soon, setting themselves up for reinjury. Psychological pressures also arise from negative teaching practices, whether through humiliation or being asked to perform in pain.

Many overachievers push past their limitations because they're never satisfied with their work. I know a twenty-six-year-old modern dancer with a well-known company who calls herself "lazy" if she doesn't put out 110 percent. By the time I saw her, she was physically ill with ulcerative colitis (a bowel disease exacerbated by stress). If you're using negative self-talk even when you're in pain, it's time to review the cognitive techniques in Chapter Six.

Responding appropriately when a physical problem occurs is also important. What do most dancers do? My research shows that nine out of ten dancers (89 percent) try to handle their injuries alone, 60 percent seek medical help only when they can't dance full-out, and almost half (49 percent) continue to work in spite of being injured. Here's a letter from a young female dancer who took this approach:

> For the last three months, I've had a problem in my left arch. Sometimes my foot hurts so much I can't point it or go up in relevé. I've been icing it three times a day, taking

*Advil, and using soothing cream before class. Nothing*
*works. You're my last hope.*

No, the orthopedist is your last hope. Whenever you have an
injury that won't go away, it's important to get an opinion from a
dance medicine specialist. Right now, you've done everything you
can. Why not get some professional help? Because injuries are so
disruptive to a dancer's lifestyle, in the next section I focus on coping strategies during the various stages of recovery.

## Treatment and Prevention

You've just sprained your ankle. Now what do you do? Although an
acute injury is always unexpected, most people can adjust after they
get used to their crutches, crack a few morbid jokes, and ask friends
to cover their casts with graffiti. This isn't the case for dancers. The
stakes are completely different when your livelihood, not to mention your self-esteem, depends on peak performance. Still, there's
no need to panic. Dancers who take a practical approach to their
recovery can often return even better than before. Dance medicine
is a growing specialty in a variety of disciplines. This means that it's
easier to have your needs met, especially if you're coming back to
dance from a serious injury. Further on, I review specific strategies
for injury prevention. This section looks at the psychology of injured dancers and the successful rehabilitation of a sprained ankle—
the most common injury in dance.

### Getting a Diagnosis

All sprained ankles are not created equal. In fact, the degree of injury can vary dramatically, so it's important to get a correct diagnosis from your orthopedist. This doctor will rate your sprain, based
on the damage to three ligaments as grade I (a mild stretch with no
joint instability), grade II (a partial tear with some instability), or

grade III (a complete tear with gross instability). Early active use and rehabilitation are the treatments of choice for grade I and II sprains. A grade III sprain could require surgery and about three months to heal.

## The Injured Psyche

"Jessica" is a serious eighteen-year-old modern dance student who got a grade II sprain after twisting her ankle in class. The damage to her body hurt, but the most disturbing element was being on the sidelines. Like many of her friends, Jessica's self-esteem depended on being a good dancer. She'd proven her devotion to dance over the years by giving up sports, Girl Scouts, and partying. Because this dancer didn't separate who she was from what she did, the injury made her feel as though she'd lost her identity.

Another loss that affected Jessica was being separated from the dance community. Before her injury, she and her friends took two classes a day, rehearsing for several hours in the afternoon for the annual workshop. Without hobbies or friends to fall back on outside of dance, Jessica felt isolated from others. She called me up in tears, saying she couldn't face recovering from her injury alone.

Dancers who're injured or ill often experience mental strain, becoming anxious or depressed. This reaction may be transient or incapacitating, depending on your ability to cope effectively. When I saw Jessica, she was avoiding rehab and felt like a failure. Some dancers may also start to overeat and gain weight or resort to substance abuse to deal with their feelings of dread. Fortunately, it's possible to take a positive approach to recovery, using the injury as a catalyst for personal renewal. Let's consider how.

## Coping Mechanisms

How you look at your injury will have a profound effect on your ability to cope with this problem. If you generally expect good things to happen, you're an optimist. Unlike pessimists, who expect the worst-case scenario, you have high self-esteem, feel more in control over what happens to you, and experience less mental strain. You also use a number of effective strategies to keep going, including reframing your injury in a more positive light. Jessica was a pessimist who worried, feeling constantly blue and on edge. To help her change her outlook, I taught her the mental skills described in Chapter Six to make it easier to navigate the various stages of recovery that accompany every serious injury.

## Stage 1: Set Realistic Goals

A sudden injury catches you off guard, whether it's a sprain or a broken bone. Your first reaction is often shock. You think: "What happened?" Jessica couldn't grasp that her world had suddenly changed, even though she was unable to walk. Though her shock wore off a few hours later at the orthopedist's office, her denial of the severity of her grade II ankle sprain didn't. Denial helps you to adapt at this stage by preserving your self-concept, while letting you hope for a swift recovery. This defense only becomes a problem if it fails to diminish over time, or it keeps you from seeking appropriate treatment.

Jessica began to face the meaning of the injury on her life over the next few weeks. As the reality of her injury sunk in, Jessica experienced a period of mourning—a normal reaction to loss—that left her withdrawn and unmotivated. I knew that she needed a lot of attention, so we focused on getting her support from family and friends. It also helps for you to settle down into a reassuring treatment routine with other injured dancers.

The primary task at this stage is to set goals that are compatible with your present level of functioning. This means that dancing isn't an option in other than grade I sprains. Jessica had a severe sprain that required that she rest with her "toes above the nose" for a few days before starting rehab with an air splint (air-padded brace) for ankle support. Fortunately, she could attend a photography course once she was on crutches. This was something that she'd always wanted to do but had never had the time. If you prefer to be around dancers while recovering from an injury, you can observe class, take notes on how others apply corrections effectively, analyze your own technique in light of what you learn, or study roles by watching a choreographer. Modern dancers may even be able to assist in choreography when their injury permits. By setting realistic goals, it's easier to adjust to the many profound changes affecting your body image, lifestyle, and abilities.

This is also a time when you should eat less to prevent your weight from becoming a problem. Because treatment options vary with each injury, it may be several weeks before you can engage in even moderate aerobic exercise, such as swimming. As a result, the best defense against weight gain is to eat fewer calories and less fat. Even though Jessica knew about healthy weight loss practices, she decided to visit a nutritionist on a regular basis for additional support.

### Stage 2: Enjoy the Small Victories

Jessica's frame of mind began to improve during the middle phase of rehab, as I helped her to appreciate the first tangible signs of progress. Dancers who can't cope with their physical limitations at this time may experience psychological problems. Obvious signs of trouble include depression or substance abuse, yet I know some dancers whose suffering seems to get lost because the signs are subtle: They may gain weight, become highly irritable, or procrastinate during rehab. Psychotherapy can be especially helpful with these problems.

Learn to enjoy each of the small victories associated with healing, such as performing extra repetitions in rehab. You also need to be prepared to handle physical discomfort, because experiencing a certain amount of pain and stiffness, and minor setbacks along the way, is normal. This is one area where Jessica had trouble, due to a low threshold for pain. She would then become anxious, which only increased her physical discomfort, creating a vicious cycle. I gave Jessica the tools to reduce her physiological arousal while stretching the scar tissue around her ankle with deep breathing exercises. She also relied on mental skills to change her perception of imminent danger. Rather than thinking the worst (I'm sure to reinjure myself"), she was objective and focused on positive thoughts ("Relax and concentrate on the exercise").

You can also use this phase to focus on body conditioning to avoid getting out of shape. Besides rehab, dancers have a wide choice of options, including Pilates-based exercises, the Alexander and Feldenkrais techniques, and aerobics that restore stamina and maintain low weight. I also referred Jessica to a special remedial class for injured dancers, where she could evaluate faulty work habits. The more you're able to analyze your bad habits, the better your chances of improving. By directing your attention to healthy avenues of pursuit, you can feel more secure and be less likely to focus on the possibly negative consequences of the injury to your dancing. Remember, many dancers sustain injuries during the course of their careers, but most of them recover and go on to new heights of accomplishment.

### Stage 3: Maintain Full Recovery

The last phase of injury rehabilitation is self-sustaining. Jessica returned to dance class, and it was clear that she would eventually be able to perform in her school's annul workshop. She was at her ideal weight, and she felt fully reconditioned and ready to discard old habits. Unfortunately, many dancers get into trouble at this stage by returning prematurely to a full schedule of dancing. Please don't do this to yourself. Your injury is still in recovery!

You can also get into problems in this final phase by cutting back on your physical therapy. Doing so can easily sabotage all of your efforts as you regain full stamina and coordination. Again, you need to set realistic goals to avoid reinjury, based on your physician's advice. To curb your frustration, stay close to prior systems of support, such as physical or Pilates-based therapy, where there's minimal stress from competition.

Another potential problem for injured professionals during recovery is losing valued roles to others. Time will most likely rectify this loss, too, as long as you're patient and remain injury-free. Jessica ended up with a better role in her workshop because of a stronger technique. Meanwhile, you can enjoy being back with your friends and the rewarding routine of dance.

As you can see, injured dancers are vulnerable to psychological stress. Fortunately, you can make an injury into a constructive experience by adapting to the various stages of recovery. If you find that you're unable to cope effectively with anxiety or depression, get a psychotherapist to help you through the rehabilitation process. Remember, it's possible to turn adversity into triumph with the right approach to injury rehabilitation. After your return, you can dance even better than before.

## Injury Prevention

Now that you know what it takes to recover from an injury, let's review how to prevent them from happening in the first place. Though only one in three dancers say they get injury prevention seminars in their dance school, there's a lot you can do on your own.

### Do a Good Warm-Up

The best way to prevent injuries is through a good warm-up. And it's never too soon to start! Unfortunately, I see far too many dancers plop down into a side split, stretching their cold, stiff bodies. Never stretch until you are warm! The goal is to progress slowly from simple to more complex movements that (1) increase your body temperature, blood flow, heart rate, and rate of breathing; (2) use the range of motion in your neck, shoulders, back, hips, knees, and feet to increase suppleness; and (3) include steps needed for balance, timing, and muscular control.

The ballet *barre* is a wonderful way to warm up for all kinds of dancers, assuming a comfortable, turned-out position. Omit *grands pliés* in first and fifth, as these place strain on the knees. I know a twenty-eight-year-old principal dancer who starts by gently jogging in place to increase circulation. Then, he sits down and does toe flexes, ankle circles, hip and spine movements, and shoulder circles before starting his *barre*. You can focus your mental attention by using any of the exercises described in Chapter Six or simply rest your mind.

## Stretching

Regular stretching (after you're warm and to help you cool down) can also prevent injuries by reducing stiffness in your joints and muscles. The way that you stretch is important, however. I know a twenty-one-year-old jazz dancer with tight calves who developed Achilles tendinitis by lunging in dance class. Ballistic stretching (bouncing) tightens your muscles rather than elongating them. Pushing too hard will also tear muscle fibers, leading to bleeding and scar tissue. Another common mistake is to overstretch certain muscle groups while leaving others out entirely. This can result in muscle imbalances.

A better approach is to lengthen each muscle group slowly while keeping the rest of the body stable. Hold the position for twenty seconds, using your breathing to help. Remember, it's not how hard you stretch—it's how often. It's also important to be thorough. Don't just do splits and forward bends. You need to stretch the turnout muscles, the front of the thighs, and the inside and back of the legs, as well as the waist, back, and shoulder muscles. Take it easy if you're sore and stiff; your muscles are probably filled with fluid and more resistant to stretching. Finally, standing on a stretch box (a wedge-shaped platform) for a few minutes several times a day may reduce your chance of developing Achilles tendinitis. Always keep proper placement during stretches. For example, don't let your feet roll in while stretching your calves. For more specific stretches, see *Stretching* in the Resource Directory.

## Listen to Your Body

Pay attention to how you feel: "Good" pain, such as a sore muscle, can mean that you're breaking new ground. The "bad" kind (it doesn't go away) leads to problems. If your body signals that it's had enough, *listen:* You may prevent a serious injury! Here's a letter from a dancer who learned this lesson the hard way:

> *I fell during an audition and really hurt my right foot. Three hours later I finally stopped dancing and got an X-ray. My fifth metatarsal was broken! Dancing through the pain was a mistake. I didn't get the part, and I may have caused even more damage to my foot. I hope other dancers can learn from my experience. We need to be a lot more careful.*

I hope that more dancers learn that it's a lot smarter to take care of an injury when it happens than it is to ignore it. In the short run, you may have to lose a role. In the long run, you don't have to risk a more serious injury.

According to dance medicine specialists, acute problems require RICE, an acronym for *rest, ice, compression* (with an Ace bandage), and *elevation*. You may also need to visit an orthopedist, get an X-ray, or go on anti-inflammatory medications. Don't self-medicate. Dancers who use too much aspirin or Advil can develop ulcers or can bruise more easily due to thinning blood. Physical problems due to overuse respond best to modified activities that favor the problem. If you work full-out even when it hurts, you can aggravate the affected area, leading to a chronic injury over time.

For more information on dance medicine, check out a two-part video series for dancers, teachers, and practitioners (see the Resource Directory). The producer, Susan Macaluso, uses top professionals in the field to identify, treat, and prevent dance injuries. The first video offers a general introduction to dance medicine; the second one gives you an in-depth look at physical problems via an actual orthopedic examination.

In the next section, we take a look at dancers' general health. Though dancers' injury rates are higher than average, there are many benefits to regular exercise and low body weight. It's also possible to work with common illnesses, such as asthma, so you can continue to dance.

## Dancers' General Health

Exercise has a positive effect on your bone density, stamina, and weight. It also does wonders for your brain by feeding it nutrients in the form of glucose and increasing nerve connections, making it easier to learn. How do dancers compare to most Americans, of whom 30 percent are completely sedentary? My research shows that dancers take an average of six dance classes a week; 79 percent do additional exercises three days a week. The most obvious result is a lower weight. On average, dancers are 6 percent below their ideal weight for height. Still, even with these benefits, some dancers face certain health problems.

### Are You Satisfied with Your Health?

The majority of dancers in my survey are "very" (41 percent) or "somewhat" (56 percent) satisfied with their health. Four percent answered "not at all" in contrast to 1 percent of the general population who report fair or poor health. For the most part, dancers are moderate drinkers. The rate of cigarette smoking is 8 percent below average for those eighteen years or older, and illicit drug use is five times lower than the norm.

Asthma is high in both male and female dancers, similar to rates among elite athletes (see Table 7.2). More surprising, however, is that both sexes also report depression. This problem is usually much higher in women than in men. Eating problems are higher in female dancers. Men, on the other hand, report a greater incidence of

**Table 7.2. Health Problems in Dancers.**

| Illness | Females (percent) | Males (percent) |
|---|---|---|
| Asthma | 14 | 17 |
| Depression | 21 | 28 |
| Eating problems | 17 | 6 |
| Sexually transmitted diseases | 2 | 17 |
| HIV | 7 | 10 |

sexually transmitted diseases. Twenty-three percent of the dancers were also tested for the AIDS virus: 10 percent of the men and 7 percent of the women are HIV-positive. This number represents 2 percent of the three hundred dancers surveyed. According to an informal survey by Dance/USA (1992) of twenty-eight dance companies, HIV affected 3.5 percent of the personnel, compared with 0.6 percent of the general population.

To help you cope with these health concerns, I discuss symptoms and solutions of some of these problems in the remaining part of this chapter. For information on eating problems, check out Chapter Three.

### Asthma

Whereas it's normal to get out of breath during vigorous exercise, excessive breathlessness, coughing, wheezing, or pain and tightness in your chest may be a sign of asthma.

Asthma comes in two broad categories. Extrinsic asthma commonly occurs after you're exposed to allergens, beginning as a child or adolescent. The other category, known as intrinsic asthma, can emerge in adults after an upper respiratory tract infection. A specific form of asthma brought on by exercise is associated with vigorous activity (running, cycling, dancing) in cold dry air or in the presence of environmental pollution. Though psychologic factors, like stress, can bring on an asthma attack, they won't produce this disorder in someone without bronchial hyperreactivity.

I know a thirty-two-year-old modern dancer who's learned to take precautions. He has no problem dancing. According to physicians, proper self-management begins by monitoring your airway functioning regularly using a peak flow meter. This reveals the severity of your condition better than the symptoms of an asthma attack. Always keep the appropriate medication nearby, and know how to respond if you fail to obtain relief or your peak flow rates drop significantly.

Dr. John Olichney, the medical consultant for the School of American Ballet, also recommends that dancers with exercise-induced asthma use their inhalers before they work out to prevent problems. All asthmatic dancers should inform their teacher of the condition and request permission to stop dancing when they feel the need. With the right approach, this inflammatory condition won't keep you out of action. In 1984, fully 11 percent of the American athletes in the Summer Olympics had a history of exercise-induced asthma. Not only is it possible to have a normal dance career with asthma, you can also excel.

## Mood Disorders

Because depression was a major complaint, I wondered whether dancers are more vulnerable to mood problems than the average person. The lifetime risk for a major depressive disorder in community samples ranges from 10 to 15 percent for women and from 5 to 12 percent for men. In my survey, 9 percent of the female dancers and 20 percent of the males said that a physician had given them a clinical diagnosis of depression. I also found that professional dancers are significantly more depressed than other dancers (19 percent versus 8 percent). A seventeen-year-old national ballet dancer came to see me in tears. She was having trouble adjusting to company life and had become depressed.

The problem with depression is that it often sneaks up on you. Some of the hidden signs to look out for include fatigue, problems with sleep, changes in appetite, and unexplained physical pain. Worrying and irritability are also common complaints, as are problems with memory and concentration.

Serious depression can make you feel hopeless about the future. In my survey, one out of three dancers have thought about suicide and 2 percent have made a serious attempt. Male dancers, and those who enter a professional career, are at greater risk for depression than average.

What can you do? If you're depressed, it's important to get professional help. Effective treatment often includes a trial of antidepressants in conjunction with psychotherapy. For more information on depression, call for a free brochure from the National Institute of Mental Health at (800) 421–4211.

## Acquired Immunodeficiency Syndrome

AIDS is an infectious disease that weakens your immune system, although it can lie dormant in your cells for up to fourteen years. The infection starts with HIV, which is the human immunodeficiency virus. AIDS is contagious. Yet you won't catch it from holding hands, hugging, or breathing the same air as an HIV-infected person. Sexual contact, however, is another story.

Most people catch the AIDS virus from an exchange of bodily fluids during sex with an infected partner. Although practicing abstinence or safe sex with the right kind of condoms helps prevent transmission, studies show that many young, sexually active people aren't taking precautions. Why not? According to Dr. Olichney, a hematologist who sees AIDS patients, heterosexuals often believe that they aren't at risk for HIV, even though infected men are transmitting this disease to women at rising rates. Gay or bisexual men, in contrast, may have a false sense of security from improved drug treatments. The other common way to catch AIDS is from contaminated blood, particularly among intravenous drug users who don't use clean needles.

Without adequate protection during sex, people are also at risk for catching a sexually transmitted disease (STD), making them more vulnerable to AIDS. Symptoms to watch out for in STDs include pain, itching, discharge, lesions, and warts. It's also important to have an annual exam if you're sexually active, because many people with STDs are asymptomatic.

If you become infected with HIV, it will take from two to six months or longer (in rare cases) for your body to manufacture antibodies to the virus. If you suspect that you've been exposed to HIV, get tested! Early treatment from an AIDS specialist can often keep the virus from multiplying and destroying white blood cells, known as T-helper or CD4 lymphocytes. Otherwise, your CD4 count may eventually drop below 200, making you vulnerable to opportunistic infections, such as pneumocystis pneumonia and cytomegalovirus (a herpes-related virus causing blindness).

Presently, AIDS treatment involves a minimum of three drugs, combining the new protease inhibitors with the older drugs like AZT. These cocktails can cause the virus in the body to diminish so that it's virtually undetectable. The resulting problem is a low compliance rate. People who feel good stop taking their medications because they don't like the side effects. When this happens, the virus develops a resistance to the drugs, so it's important to stick with your regimen.

A twentieth-century plague, AIDS has caused the loss of loved ones across the globe, as well as many talented dancers, teachers, directors, and choreographers in the dance community. My research shows that 32 percent (one out of three) of dancers know someone with the HIV virus and 37 percent know someone who's died of an AIDS-related illness.

Yet many dancers simply avoid the topic. Ian Betts, a modern dancer who also counsels AIDS patients as a deacon, says, "Dance is such a body-oriented profession that you're ostracized when you're sick. No one wants to deal with disabilities, so when it happens, you're left alone." In my survey, 60 percent of the dancers with HIV told their colleagues. Only one out of three received emotional support!

Dancers who've been infected with AIDS don't have to deal with it alone. The Actor's Fund of America (800–221–7303) has a full-scale AIDS initiative for entertainers who've worked in the business. They offer a range of social services from mental health counseling to support groups and referrals for legal assistance. Low-income dancers may also receive direct subsidies for food, rent, utilities, and medical care. Ulysses Dove, the late choreographer, received help from the Actor's Fund when he was struck down with AIDS, penniless, and without health insurance. Dancers who are members of a performing arts union should also check with their union for any services or referrals.

AIDS is a chronic disease, but it no longer means a death sentence if you get an early start with the right course of treatment. For more information on service organizations and prevention brochures, contact the Center for Disease Control's twenty-four-hour hotline (800–342–AIDS) or check out Garwood and Melnick's book *What Everyone Can Do to Fight AIDS* (see the Further Reading section).

## Health Insurance

Let's look at your options. Right now, insurance is a big issue for a lot of dancers. Few dance companies can pay for it, and workers' compensation doesn't always cover the problem. Twenty-one percent of professional dancers have no coverage, compared to 6 percent of the rest of the sample, which consists of ex-dancers and students. If you don't have health insurance, consider joining the Dance Professionals Associates—a new organization that offers low-cost premiums to all dancers and their families (see the Resource

Directory). There are also more than twenty performing arts health clinics throughout the country that offer services on a reduced or sliding scale.

———————

Musculoskeletal injuries are often an inevitable part of the achievement process in dance, in which you're both artist and athlete. The more you know about the causes of dance injuries, the better position you'll be in to prevent serious problems. How you choose to respond to a dance injury will also affect the process of recovery. Though much of this chapter focuses on solving problems, it's important to remember that dancers are some of the healthiest people around. My goal is to ensure your continued health and well-being by giving you the facts.

In the final chapter, I discuss the dancer in transition. Often, there's a mourning process as you let go of this identity. Although leaving dance is never easy, I know that it's possible to find meaning in the next phase of your life. To help you make the most of this change, we look at why some dancers are forced out of the profession rather than choosing to leave. I also tell you about transition centers for dancers that offer career counseling, scholarships, and seminars. It is possible to bridge the gap to the next phase of your life!

# $\mathscr{I}$s There Life After Dance?

$\mathscr{O}$nce you stop being a dancer, then what? If you're caught off guard, you suffer culture shock—big time! I know dancers who've been traumatized when problems like injuries or joblessness forced them out after years of devotion. On the other hand, dancers who make a transition to something new and meaningful often have an easier time. Still, many say that leaving dance is "like losing my best friend."

This chapter examines life after dance for students and professionals. There's no road map to follow, yet you can take the next step with the right approach. To accomplish this task smoothly, you need to counter the factors that force dancers out of this art form; prepare to enter the next stage of your life; and address the feelings of grief that surround this loss.

## Avoiding Premature Losses

The dance profession requires almost total immersion. This sacrifice is worth it if dance is your top priority. If it isn't, the chances are that you'll quit before dancing takes over your life. Research shows that gifted students who put socializing first rarely develop their talent to its fullest. On the other hand, devoted dance students stick it out—for better or for worse.

Over time, these students often become overly invested in the dancer identity. Yet the reality is that dancing is a precarious profession. Any number of factors can and will force you out, including burnout, unemployment, injuries, and age. While some of these problems aren't under your control, there's a lot you can do to help yourself.

### Preventing Burnout

Are you driven? Goal-oriented? A perfectionist? Is each day a test of your abilities? If you're not careful, you may be headed for a serious case of burnout. Dancers who lead one-track lives often fizzle out. Some get completely disenchanted and flee the profession, whereas others push themselves until they're exhausted. Here's an example:

"Denise," a talented twenty-four-year-old modern dancer, believed that she had to toil nonstop if she wanted to make it in New York. Instead of scheduling downtime with friends or giving in to fatigue, this dancer devoted her entire life to goal-oriented activities: she did dance class, rehearsals, and aerobic exercise during the day; washed her laundry and shopped for groceries in the evening; and cleaned her (neat) apartment before going to bed. Yet no matter how much effort she put out, she was going nowhere fast. The director of her junior dance company ignored her, and she spent all of her free time home alone with her cat.

By the time Denise came to see me, she was burned out. We slowly began to reverse the problem with rest, relaxation exercises, and fun activities. I also taught her cognitive techniques (see Chapter Six) to counter the negative thoughts that arose whenever she took a break. Two months later, her director noticed a happier, more energetic dancer in class and recommended that she audition for the first company.

## Detecting Burnout

Denise's experience is a typical case of burnout. She thought she could handle anything, and denied herself R&R until she was mentally and physically exhausted. Though this dancer recovered, she still has to guard against making too many demands on her time and energy. To discover whether you're a candidate for burnout, see if you've undergone any of the following changes over the past six months. These symptoms, adapted from a self-test developed by Dr. Herbert Freudenberger, are included in his book with Geraldine Richelson, *Burn-Out: The High Cost of High Achievement.*

- You're so busy you can't even do routine tasks like send out Christmas cards or return phone calls.

- You tire easily, finding it difficult to bounce back after a stressful period at work.

- You're working harder and harder but feel like you're accomplishing less and less.

- It's difficult to remember deadlines, appointments, or even where you left stuff, like your wallet or keys.

- There's no joy in your life. Not only can't you take a joke, but you feel increasingly disillusioned, sad, irritable, or disappointed with others.

- Your body's out of whack, leading to problems such as chest pains, headaches, stomach aches, skin disorders, back pains, or lingering colds.

- You feel disoriented when the work of the day stops.

- Friends and family are getting on your nerves, telling you that you don't look so good.

- You've stopped socializing and have little to say to others.

- Sex is now more trouble than it's worth.

Is it time to rekindle your flame? Be aware that denial is a major coping mechanism for people who develop burnout. Yet no one is superhuman. If you can admit this to yourself, you'll be in a better position to increase your personal resources. Let's see how.

1. Research shows that having fun with a friend is the best antidote to burnout. High achievers need to create a balance between work and play, adding activities with no purpose other than enjoyment.

2. Stop trying to be perfect. Everyone makes mistakes. Some are important; others aren't a big deal. Find out where you have some leeway, then take it!

3. Ask for help when you need it, including quenching your thirst for recognition. For example, if you need a pat on the back for a job well done, let someone special know.

4. Pace yourself at work. Something as simple as taking several fifteen-minute breaks throughout the day can make all the difference in the world to your well-being.

Remember, you don't have to push yourself nonstop to excel. So, before you burn out, take some time out—and have fun!

### Finding a Dance Job

Another occupational hazard that can boot you out of dance is unemployment. Many dance students tell me their dream is to become professionals. Yet finding a dance job is tough. I know an eighteen-year-old ballet dancer who bailed out after three months of intensive auditions, whereas her nineteen-year-old roommate attended every open call in musical theater for over a year. Neither found a job. Does anything work?

While there's no guarantee in any profession, much less in dance, it pays to a have a plan of action. If you don't, joblessness may stop you in your tracks years before dancers' usual age of retirement in their mid-thirties. Check out Chapter Five for more on specific job-hunting strategies in dance. You can also benefit by following these tips.

1. Use several methods—networking, audition tours, company directories—to get a dance position. If you limit yourself to going to open calls, it won't be enough. However, don't go overboard using five or six methods, either, or you won't be able to give each one the time it deserves.

2. Be persistent, and contact many dance companies or shows. But first be sure you're prepared mentally and financially for an extensive search. I've known dancers who got a performing job in four months or less, but I've known others who took two years. Reread Chapter Five to find survival work and Chapter Six to keep rejections from beating you down. Remember, every time you show up for an audition, you're a winner.

3. Set your sights on small dance companies, not just the big ones with a roster of stars. It's easier to approach a small group with fifteen or twenty dancers, and you're more likely to get hired. One dancer quit the profession at age seventeen when the New York City Ballet didn't hire her. Fifteen years later, she realizes that she could have been happy in a regional dance company.

4. Know that your attitude, not just your ability to dance, will play a role in getting you a position as a performer. A beautiful eighteen-year-old dancer learned this lesson the hard way. Intent on playing it cool in an important audition, she ended

up looking bored and sullen. Her equally talented friend radiated enthusiasm despite a slight weight problem. Guess who got the job. (I think you already know it wasn't the one with the bad attitude.)

So, all you dancers who want to perform, remember to use several job-hunting methods, persevere, and consider small dance companies. And watch your attitude! Dancers who put up walls, distancing themselves from possible rejection, increase their chances of that very rejection. Yet it can also backfire if you overcompensate by projecting a forced gaiety. To let your true personality and gifts shine through in any audition, use the mental skills in Chapter Six. Dance jobs are out there waiting to be filled. It's up to you to find them.

### Musculoskeletal Injuries

So far, we've discussed how to reduce your chances of burnout and unemployment; however, this advice is only useful if you're healthy enough to perform. Though a serious career-ending injury is rare in dance, cumulative wear and tear on the body affects everyone—even if you're only taking dance class for fun. What's the price of being steadfast to the bitter end?

My research shows that dancing for eighteen years or longer leads to more injuries in every category than dancing for only a decade. Dancers who keep at this activity have significantly more tendinitis, stress fractures, chronic injuries, and arthritis. I know a serious forty-year-old dance student who was devastated after she developed an arthritic knee. It wasn't the pain so much as the fact that she could no longer take dance class. She's now making the difficult transition with a Pilates-based program for dancers, where she can build strength and flexibility without stressing her joints.

A debilitating injury exacts an even higher toll on professionals who face an early retirement. Dancers with chronic tendinitis quit at the age of thirty-two—eleven years before performers without such injuries! Foot problems are equally worrisome for dancers, leading to retirement at age thirty. Dancing is extremely athletic, so injuries are to be expected. Still, the only way you can stop the build-up of physical problems is by taking a proactive approach to injury prevention.

In Chapter Seven, I tell you about the benefits of warming up, stretching, and distinguishing good pain (a sign of progress) from the bad pain that signals damage. You can also reduce overuse, the most common cause of injuries in dancers, by monitoring your work schedule. Here are some suggestions from dance medicine specialists.

Pay attention to the warning signs of overtraining! Overtraining occurs when there's an imbalance between exercise and recovery. Obvious symptoms include feeling uncoordinated, tired, sore, and sluggish. One twenty-two-year-old dance student with these symptoms thought she was getting out of shape. As a result, she increased her work output from two to four dance classes a day. This tactic reduced her recovery time even further, creating persistent fatigue—and tendinitis in her ankles.

Prevention of overuse injuries begins by scheduling time-out from exercise. Plan rest days during the week, as well as "easy" weeks over long periods of training. Each time you finish exercising, take five to fifteen minutes to warm-down and stretch, a habit that reduces fatigue and muscle soreness. Regular massage and whirlpools also help soft tissues recover from strenuous exercise. Last but not least, sleep is important. Dancers who're training hard may need ten to twelve hours of sleep each night. When in doubt, take a catnap.

If you let your work schedule get away from you, symptoms of overtraining may appear. At this point, the best solution is to spend forty-two to seventy-eight hours in bed. I know a twenty-three-year-old jazz dancer who spent an entire weekend in bed after an intensive two-week tour. She returned to class feeling full of beans. If you don't recover after a short period of bed rest, you may have the overtraining syndrome. This problem won't go away overnight. In fact, it can take weeks, or even months, to recover. A nineteen-year-old ballet dancer who came down with this syndrome noticed a decrease in performance ability, overuse injuries, loss of appetite, depression, and other signs of trouble. It took her two months to recover with proper treatment, which included rest, physical therapy, attention to diet, and psychological support.

As you can see, the body needs time to snap back from intense periods of exercise. Athletic coaches are now more alert to the symptoms of overtraining, adjusting their athletes' training load accordingly. It's time for the dance world to do the same.

**The Older Dancer**

Dance is a youth-oriented profession. Ballet dancers start working in their late teens, whereas jazz and modern dancers often begin in their early twenties. While no one can prevent the march of time, you can affect how you age. It pays to be aware of what lies ahead.

Experts tell us that the human body is designed to last 110 years. Yet few people make it to this age. Typically, your body begins a slow decline in your twenties and thirties. The good news is that many problems associated with aging can be prevented or reversed. Here's what can happen if you do nothing.

Research shows that there's a gradual decline in aerobic capacity after age twenty-five. Over the next fifty years, the heart will shrink and beat more slowly, the blood vessels will narrow, and systolic blood pressure will rise (the top number on the gauge). Cardiovascular changes make it easier to get winded with exertion.

Bones, joints, and muscles also begin to age. First, there's a slow but steady decline in bone density and strength as calcium leaves the body after age thirty-five. In the forties, some joint stiffness may appear in the neck, knees, and hips. Muscle strength, which is at its peak in the thirties, also begins to deteriorate: the number of muscle fibers shrinks and fat deposits expand. Metabolism slows down. By the age of seventy, the body requires 500 fewer calories to survive.

Older dancers can offset many of these problems with a healthy diet, low-impact aerobics, moderate use of alcohol, weight training, and no smoking. For example, while exercise won't effect the number of decreasing muscle fibers, it can increase the size of each fiber, adding to your strength. Aerobic exercises can improve cardiovascular fitness and speed up your metabolism, although you may need to take more breaths. Meanwhile, weight-bearing exercise will protect your bones, along with a diet rich in calcium. (Women should check out hormone-replacement therapy if they aren't menstruating.) Adopt a healthy lifestyle and you'll also keep down your weight and blood pressure.

As you age, your warm-up in dance should be longer, with shorter periods of total layoff. It's also important to make allowances for subtle problems, such as a "glass ankle" or a "trick knee," that begin to show up in your twenties. Be aware that major injuries increase significantly in dancers after the age of thirty. I know a resilient ballerina who sprained her ankle at thirty-one—the first serious injury in her twelve-year career. After a lengthy recovery, this dancer worked hard to prevent injuries. She retired at thirty-nine to have a baby.

### When Do Most Professional Dancers Retire?

The answer depends on your standing in the dance world. If you haven't been promoted by your mid-twenties, a major career is unlikely to happen. Companies may then begin to nudge you out by taking away cherished roles. A dancer may also choose to leave for something with greater rewards. Whatever the reason, my research shows that corps dancers retire, on average, eleven years earlier than principals (twenty-nine versus forty years old). Soloists retire at the age of thirty-five. At this point, dancers may start families or another line of work. Only a few middle-aged professionals continue to perform on their own. Dancers who fall into this minority can find out about performing opportunities by contacting a group called Dancers over 40 (see the Resource Directory).

# After You Quit Dancing

So far we've focused on factors that push students and profession-als out of dance. Now that you know what to watch out for, take some time to prepare for your inevitable transition. Otherwise, you may feel as though someone's just pulled the rug from under your feet. Here's what you need to do.

## Preparation Is Key

How do you plan for the future? Start early! Career experts agree that it's better to make a gradual transition than to switch to some-thing new out of the blue. To take this one step at a time, you need to answer these questions:

- "What do I want to do?"

- "Where do I want to do it?"

- "How do I get the necessary training?"

There are twenty thousand different jobs in the United States, so it's easy to get overwhelmed. I'll take you through the basic steps to find a job that's right for you.

In Chapter Five, I suggest that you do a personal inventory to find a survival job, based on your interests, abilities, and personal-ity. This information is especially useful for a career transition. Un-fortunately, I know dancers who spend more time planning next summer's vacation than they do a second career. They say, "If it's meant to be, it'll just happen." While this strategy may have led you to your first love (dance), it's risky. After all, you're trying to replace your old passion with something new and meaningful.

Let's take a look at your choices. According to vocational coun-selors, every career involves a domain (like dance) and a job de-scription (performer). When it's time to shift gears, you have three options.

1. You can switch your domain but keep the same job description. I know a thirty-three-year-old dancer who made this career transition by switching to acting (new domain) while remaining a performer (same job description).

2. You can switch the name of your job but stay in the same domain. Many dancers do this when they go into teaching.

3. You can change both, entering a different domain with a completely different job description. I did this by switching to psychology and becoming a therapist, specializing in performers. Other possible new domains for dancers include performing arts law, medicine, and physical therapy.

To make any career change, you will need experience and, possibly, extra training. Managing your time is important. It took me eight years to complete college and graduate school—the same amount of time to master dance! Of course, you can also develop your skills through hobbies, survival work, or internships. The sooner you begin, the more prepared you'll be for your next career. Otherwise, you may have to take whatever you can get, like this next dancer.

"Robert" is a thirty-five-year-old modern dancer who'd risen to the top of his profession after graduating from a college dance program. Then, he ruptured a knee ligament, thus ending a career in a good modern dance company. Like many serious dancers, he had no idea what he wanted to do next, so he impulsively jumped at the nearest job, which happened to be teaching. The problem was that he hated it. He was also grieving the loss of his first career, beginning a necessary but painful mourning process, which I cover at length at the end of this chapter. Robert felt like he was in limbo for the next twelve months.

As he slowly came to terms with his conflicting emotions, he decided to explore a long-standing interest in choreography. He got an M.F.A. in dance at the local university, eventually returning to his former company to create dance pieces. After several years of favorable reviews, he was ready to venture out on his own, successfully choreographing for dance companies in America and Europe.

The moral of the story: Know what you want to do before you throw yourself into something else. Then, get the training to do it. Here are some of the *wrong* ways to choose a new career:

- On a whim or an impulse

- After a casual conversation

- Based on a news broadcast

- To work near a boyfriend or girlfriend

- Following in a parent's footsteps

To stay with the example of teaching dance for a moment longer, let's suppose you know you want to be a teacher after filling in at your local dance studio. You've answered the question *what*. Now, you have to move on to the question of *where* you'd like to do it, to answer the last question of *how* to do it.

For example, many dance academies prefer that you train at a well-known dance school or be a seasoned performer. In contrast, arts magnet schools require a bachelor's degree in dance, experience as a student teacher, and certification by your local board of education. A master's degree may enable you to teach in a university. Although I know a few ex-performers who've gained substitute certification without a higher degree, don't count on it.

### Starting Your Own Business

The more you know about where you want to work, the more you can learn about how to do it. This advice also applies to starting your own business. If it's a dance school, you'll need to find a commercial space that's convenient to reach by subway or car. A dance studio's size, appearance, and the quality of the floor are also important.

The next step involves a lot of paperwork, such as starting a business account, registering in your state, and contacting the IRS. If you aren't familiar with setting up a business, take a course at your local university or consult a small-business advisory service. Eighty-five percent of small businesses fail within the first three years because of poor planning! You'll also need to attract students. Networking is an inexpensive form of marketing, though you may also want to use the services of a professional if you can afford the expense. Just remember to start small. It takes time to build a reputation in the community.

## Other Possibilities

OK, now that you know about answering the basic questions for teaching dance, let's explore other popular career options. I received the following letter from a curious dancer:

> *I've heard about a fairly new career field known as dance therapy. Could you tell me more about it?*

Dance therapy is one of several approaches that use the arts to treat people with emotional and physical problems. To qualify as a therapist, you must have training in dance and in psychology. This usually involves earning a master's degree after four years of college. Most dance therapists find work in a hospital or clinic or in private practice. For more information, call the American Dance Therapy Association (see the Resource Directory).

Another question that often comes up in letters to my advice column involves physical therapy. I'm not surprised, because many injured dancers have been in rehab. I know a thirty-six-year-old dancer who was drawn to physical therapy as she underwent treatment for an injury. Later, she entered the field, working in a clinic for performing artists.

If you choose this route, apply to a number of physical therapy programs, because the competition is stiff. You'll need to earn a high grade-point average, as well as meet certain prerequisites, especially in the sciences. A master's degree offers more advanced training than a bachelor of science; however, both degrees will qualify you for state licensing. The American Physical Therapy Association offers a list of undergraduate and graduate programs across the country (see the Resource Directory).

Many dancers also express interest in jobs that keep them employed in a dance company but in a capacity other than performer. In this case, you might consider a position in public relations, fundraising, arts administration, or education. Big dance companies, like New York City Ballet, often offer training internships with small stipends. You can also find out about job requirements by looking at *ArtSearch*, a bimonthly bulletin that lists employment opportunities in the performing arts.

Obviously, there's a lot to consider before you venture out into the real world. Some jobs will also require more training than others. Before you invest years of your life getting a higher degree, it pays to know whether there's much demand for this job. You can get an idea of the job market by asking several people in your future career about the prospects of finding work. If you still have some misgivings about taking the next step, don't worry. It's normal to be afraid of the unknown.

When I contemplated my retirement from New York City Ballet, no one was talking about second careers. Serious dancers were only supposed to be interested in dance. Fortunately, the topic of career transition is now out in the open. While it's still hard to find something else to care so much about, more dancers are thinking ahead. At the moment, over thirty-five dancers from City Ballet are attending college. Many receive funding from the Dance On Foundation, a nonprofit organization designed to help these dancers reap the benefits of a higher education.

It's also common these days for dancers to meet with vocational counselors at transition centers in Great Britain, Canada, the

United States, and the Netherlands (see the Resource Directory). In America, Career Transitions for Dancers offers free vocational testing to those who've performed a minimum of one hundred weeks over a seven-year period. A national career hotline caters to all dancers, including students who're just starting out. Finally, a valuable resource for groups wishing to start a dancer's transition center is the International Organization for the Transition of Professional Dancers. Unlike dancers of the past, you don't have to travel this route alone.

## Letting Go of Dance

The last piece of the puzzle in a career transition has to do with your reaction to leaving dance. Even though three out of five retired dancers continue to take class, switching to another career often strikes at the heart of your identity. Dance students who fail to become professionals can also face a crisis in meaning, as their dreams vanish into thin air. To make a successful transition, you need to deal with your feelings of loss before you can gain energy for a new direction.

### Life After Dance

Why is leaving dance so difficult? Elisabeth Kübler-Ross, an expert on dying, describes retirement as one of the little deaths of life. This is especially true for dancers, who approach their careers with the intensity of a religious vocation. When it's over, experiencing a mix of raw and contradictory emotions is normal. I know a thirty-nine-year-old retired dancer who fluctuated among anger, regret, relief, fear, sorrow, and euphoria. She kept these feelings to herself, believing she should handle them alone. Fortunately, this dancer finally got support in psychotherapy. After grieving for her lost vocation, she began to turn her life around.

Another factor complicating the transition process is your motivation for leaving this career. Remember, many factors can push you out of dance. As it turns out, this is a big problem for women, who report more negative reasons for leaving dance than do men. Women also outnumber men three to one in dance, with only so many jobs to go around. Retiring from dance by default is tough. I know a depressed thirty-two-year-old modern dancer who was fired after a long battle with injuries. She has no idea what she wants to do next in spite of having a college degree. It helps to know the answer to this question before leaving dance.

The final obstacle to a career transition comes from the insular existence of many dancers. Dance training often begins in childhood or early adolescence, leaving little time to experiment with different roles or identities. I know a thirty-four-year-old ballet dancer who feels trapped in adolescence. While her friends were going to parties, she spent her time in the studio, refining her technique. Now, she wonders whether she'll be able to manage in the real world. Your ability to cope with all of these stresses is important because adjusting to life after dance takes time.

**The Mourning Process**

A career transition involves a series of losses that include your workplace, community, and identity. To move forward, dancers go through a period of mourning. The stages associated with grieving include

- Coming to terms with your past

- "Letting go" of lost attachments

- Reinvesting in life after dance

Dancers who miss any of these stages may suffer from a number of psychological and physical problems, due to unresolved grief. The good news is that you can often reverse these problems, even years later, by completing the process of mourning.

## Coping with Loss

Each dancer's response to loss differs, depending on the circumstances. I've known dancers who've become preoccupied with feelings of anger, guilt, or despair, who've berated themselves for past mistakes, or blamed others for their predicament. Physically healthy dancers may also be more vulnerable to injuries at this time. While a serious injury can take the decision to retire out of your hands, it does nothing to resolve your grief.

Rather than avoiding your feelings of loss, find ways to tolerate a certain amount of crisis and despair. You need to come to terms with how much dancing means to you, as well as the cost of this devotion. Not surprisingly, this process often unleashes a wellspring of emotions. You may experience conflicting feelings for various reasons. I know a forty-two-year-old leading dancer who looks back on her highly successful career feeling that the best part of her life is over. This differs from a disillusioned twenty-nine-year-old corps dancer, whose lack of success makes it difficult to relinquish all hope for the future. Their beliefs about themselves, the world, and the future will also play a big role in how they react to a transition from dance.

Here are a few examples. Let's suppose that you believe you're only a "dancer" rather than a "person who loves to dance." This belief can keep you from exploring other career paths. Likewise, it doesn't help if your view of the world rests on the belief that power lies in the hands of others. I know a twenty-four-year-old ballet dancer who handed over all control to her artistic director, adopting a passive approach to life. Last but not least, there is the pessimistic dancer who strongly believes that life without dance is worthless and so may give up hope. A lot of my work focuses on helping dancers modify these beliefs, using the cognitive techniques outlined in Chapter Six.

## Letting Go of Dance

As you start to change your beliefs and let go of your intense attachment to dance, your focus will begin to shift from the past to the future. This may be the first time that you feel ready to tap into your resources outside of dancing. To protect yourself from disappointment, make sure that your expectations are realistic.

Remember, after spending most of your life pursuing dance, it's not likely that you'll find a new path right away. Real change requires a period of ambiguity, as you explore different interests and talents. Although the process may seem chaotic, it's normal to have conflicting feelings about your past, even as you begin to face the future.

Some dancers tell me that they're still obsessed with the past. Believe it or not, ruminating about dance is part of the healing process. Still, you may need to deal with unresolved guilt over lost career opportunities or anger at others who aren't facing a career transition. I often find that dancers procrastinate when they're anxious or depressed, fear failure, or have low self-esteem. This is when outside support is most important, as you struggle to be on your own without direction or authority.

The last part of letting go has to do with giving up symbols from the past. This may mean throwing out your dance bag or allowing yourself to gain a few pounds. Now's the time to pay attention to the work habits that'll be an asset in your career transition. Courses in arts administration helped a thirty-two-year-old dancer to move forward. I believe that all dancers also have a lot to offer a new career because of their discipline and work ethic. Try not to get caught up in a cage of self-doubt. By focusing on negative beliefs, you may ignore your full potential.

## Investing in Life After Dance

The last stage of a transition is one of recovery. You've met the biggest challenges of mourning dance and survived! Take this time to make sensible choices. A twenty-three-year-old injured dancer realized that her first job as a paralegal wasn't the best fit. After careful consideration, she switched to the restaurant business.

If you're feeling a lot of fear, it can help to visualize yourself after dance, using the mental skills outlined in Chapter Six. This visualization may also make it easier to deal with the practical aspects of a career transition when you visit a vocational counselor. As you imagine yourself in the future, you'll be more likely to adopt a strategy to handle the concrete aspects of switching careers. This includes time management, financial planning, and a realistic appraisal of the job market.

Recovery from a career transition is an ongoing process. Once you adapt to life after dance, you'll see yourself in a different way, as will others in the community. Over time, this will require additional adjustments. Luckily, it's possible to remain true to your own aspirations by cherishing the values, ideals, and standards that have governed your life in the past.

As you've seen, a dancer's career is short. Injuries and other problems can also leave you by the wayside. While there's a lot you can do to help yourself, remember to make plans for the future. It's never too early. Having developed skills that aid a career transition while exploring other interests also helps, as well as practicing time management. In this way, you'll be able to have another career if you want it. Dance companies should also take a role by sponsoring educational seminars and getting involved with career transition centers.

Finally, be prepared to address the extensive role that dancing has played in your lifestyle and identity. This process unleashes a mixture of painful and contradictory feelings that you resolve by going through the various stages of mourning. Every dancer copes differently with this profound loss. In some cases, psychotherapy may help if your self-esteem is fragile.

Dancers are often so devoted to their work that they may have eyes for nothing else. The good news is that you have a lot to offer another career. Few people work as hard or are as disciplined as dancers. The biggest challenge will be finding something else to care about. Once you do, it will be easier to let go of the dancer identity. Just remember—after every ending, there's always a new beginning.

# Resource Directory

## Agents

*Ross Reports Television and Film*
BPI Communications
1515 Broadway, 14th floor
New York, NY 10036
(212) 764–7300; (800) 817–3273

*Stern's Performing Arts Directory*
*Dance Magazine*
33 West 60th Street, 10th floor
New York, NY 10023
(212) 245–9050

## AIDS

Actors' Fund of America Social Services
1501 Broadway, Suite 518
New York, NY 10036
(212) 221–7300; (800) 221–7303

National AIDS Information Clearing House
CDC Hotline: (800) 342-AIDS
http://sunsite.unc.edu/asha

## Apparel and Health Care Products

Angelic Support Bra
c/o Angela Kostritzky
209 Columbus Avenue, #C
New York, NY 10023
(212) 579–0525

ArtsCare (health care products)
c/o Pilates Studio®
2121 Broadway, 2nd floor
New York, NY 10023
(212) 875–0189, ext. 23; (888) 278–7227

Bunheads, Inc. (footwear catalogue)
53 Church Street
Saratoga Springs, NY 12866
(518) 581–0513; (800) 311–6563

*Stern's Performing Arts Directory*
(lists businesses in dancewear, merchandise,
stage makeup, and equipment)
*Dance Magazine*
33 West 60th Street, 10th floor
New York, NY 10023
(212) 245–9050

## Career Transition Centers

### Canada

Dancer Transition Resource Centre
66 Gerrard Street East, Suite 202
Toronto, Ontario M5B 1G3
(416) 595–5655

### Netherlands

Theater Instituut Nederland
Postbus 19304
NL-1000 GH Amsterdam
31–20–551–33–00

## United Kingdom

Dance Companies Resettlement Fund and Dancers Trust
Rooms 222–227 Africa House
64–67 Kingsway
London WC2B 6BG, England
44–171–404–6141

## United States

*Nationwide*

CareerLine (National Career Transition for Dancers hotline)
(800) 581–2833

*California*

Career Transition for Dancers (CTFD)
5757 Wilshire Boulevard, 8th floor
Los Angeles, CA 90036
(213) 549–6660

*New York*

Career Transition for Dancers (CTFD)
1727 Broadway, 2nd floor
New York, NY 10019
(212) 581–7043

# Career Transition Options and Survival Jobs

## Makeup Artists

Christine Valmy International School
437 Fifth Avenue, 2nd floor
New York, NY 10016
(212) 779–7800; (800) 24-VALMY

## Physical Trainers and Therapists

American College of Sports Medicine (home-study programs)
P.O. Box 1440
Indianapolis, IN 46206
(317) 637–9200; (800) 486–5643

American Council on Exercise (home-study programs)
P.O. Box 910449
San Diego, CA 92191
(800) 825–3636
http://www.acefitness.org

American Dance Therapy Association
2000 Century Plaza, Suite 108
10636 Little Patuxent Parkway
Columbia, MD 21044
(410) 997–4040
http://www.adta.org

American Physical Therapy Association
1111 North Fairfax Street
Alexandria, VA 22314
(800) 999–2782
http://www.apta.org

Feldenkrais Guild
524 Ellsworth Street SW
Albany, OR 97321
(541) 926–0981; (800) 775–2118
http://www.feldenkrais.com

The Method® developed by Joseph Pilates
Physicalmind Institute
1807 Second Street, Suite 47
Santa Fe, NM 87505
(505) 988–1990; (800) 505–1990

North American Society of Teachers of the
Alexander Technique
3010 Hennepin Avenue South, Suite 10
Minneapolis, MN 55408
(800) 473–0620

The Pilates Studio®
890 Broadway, 6th floor
New York, NY 10003
(212) 358–7676; (800) 474–5283


The Swedish Institute
226 West 26th Street, 5th floor
New York, NY 10001
(212) 924–5900


## Competitions

International Ballet Association Luxembourg (ages 15–27)
41 rue A. Useldinger
L-4351 Esch/Alzette
Luxembourg
352–55–54–55


International Ballet Competition (ballet and modern; ages 14–25)
1102 Taylor Avenue
Baltimore, MD 21227
(410) 242–4442
http://www.erols.com/nijinsky


International Ballet Competition Maya
(ballet and modern; ages 17–26)
Off. 95, 86 Nevsky Prospekt
St. Petersburg, Russia 191025
7–812–275–4220


International Competition Alicia Alonso
(ballet, modern, folk; ages 10–27)
Centro Pro Danza
Ave. 51, No. 11805, Marianao,
La Habana, Cuba
53–7–20–8610

Prix de Lausanne (ballet and modern; ages 15–18)
Palais de Beaulieu
avenue des Bergières 6
CH-1004 Lausanne, Switzerland
41–21–643–24–05

USA International Ballet Competition (ages 15–26)
P.O. Box 3696
Jackson, MS 39207
(601) 355–9853
http://www.usaibc.com

Varna International Ballet Competition
(ballet and modern; ages 15–25)
6 Serdika Street
1000 Sofia
Bulgaria
359–2–883–377
http://www.bulgarianspace.com/music/varna_ibc

## Dance Organizations

Dance Educators of America
Vickie Sheer, Executive Director
P.O. Box 607
Pelham, NY 10803
(914) 636–3200

Dance Masters of America
Robert Mann, Executive Secretary
P.O. Box 610533
Bayside, NY 11361
(718) 225–4013

Dancers Over 40, Inc.
P.O. Box 911
New York, NY 10108
(212) 581–4475

International Association for Dance Medicine and Science
Jan Dunn, M.S., Executive Director
2555 Andrew Drive
Superior, CO 80027
(303) 494–9450

International Organization for the
Transition of Professional Dancers
Philippe Braunschweig, President
avenue des Bergières 6
CH-1004 Lausanne, Switzerland
41–21–643–24–05

National Dance Association
Jane Bonbright, Executive Director
1900 Association Drive
Reston, VA 20191
(703) 476–3436
http://www.aahperd.org/nda/nda.html

National Dance Council of America
Joy Edwards, Publications Director
407 Mill Street
Vienna, VA 22180
(703) 242–2569

## Dance Publications

### Books

*Dance Medicine and Science Bibliography*, compiled by Ruth Solomon and John Solomon (1996).

*Dance Medicine Resource Guide*, edited by Marshall Hagins (1997).
J. Michael Ryan Publishing, Inc.
24 Crescent Drive North
Andover, NJ 07821
(973) 786–7777

*Dancing Longer, Dancing Stronger*, by Andrea Watkins
and Priscilla Clarkson (1990).

*Diet for Dancers*, by Robin D. Chmelar and Sally Fitt (1990).

*The Pointe Book, Revised: Shoes, Training, and Technique*,
by Janice Barringer and Sarah Schlesinger (1997).
Princeton Book Company, Publishers
P.O. Box 831
Hightstown, NJ 08520
(609) 426–0602; (800) 220–7149
http://www.dancehorizons.com

*Stretching*, by Bob Anderson (1980).
Random House
400 Hahn Road
Westminster, MD 21157
(800) 726–0600
http://www.randomhouse.com

*What Everyone Can Do to Fight AIDS*, by Anne Garwood
and Ben Melnick (1995).
Jossey-Bass Publishers
350 Sansome Street
San Francisco, CA 94104
(415) 433–1740; (800) 956–7739
http://www.josseybass.com

## Journal

*Journal of Dance Medicine and Science*
J. Michael Ryan Publishing, Inc.
24 Crescent Drive North
Andover, NJ 07821
(973) 786–7777

**Magazines**

*Dance Europe*
P.O. Box 12661
London E5 9TZ, England
44–181–985–7767
http://www.danceeurope.co.uk

*Dance Magazine*
33 West 60th Street, 10th floor
New York, NY 10023
(212) 245–9050
http://www.dancemagazine.com

## Dance Videos

*The Balanchine Essays,* nine-part series on George Balanchine's technique.
Princeton Book Company, Publishers
P.O. Box 831
Hightstown, NJ 08520
(609) 737–8177; (800) 220–7149
http://www.dancehorizons.com

*Introduction to Dance Medicine: Keeping Dancers Dancing.*
*Lower Extremity Dance Medicine: Orthopedic Examination with*
*Dr. William Hamilton.*
Dance Medicine Educational Fund
P.O. Box 572
Jackson Heights, NY 11372
(718) 426–8606

## Eating Disorders

Overeaters Anonymous
World Service Office
6075 Zenith Court NE
Rio Rancho, NM 87124
(505) 891–2664
http://www.overeatersanonymous.org

The Renfrew Center
475 Spring Lane
Philadelphia, PA 19128
(215) 482–5353; (800) 736–3739
http://www.renfrew.org

## High School and College Dance Programs
## (Scholarship Information)

*The Bible of Performing Arts Education*, by Muriel Topaz (1998).
*Princeton Review*
2515 Broadway, 2nd floor
New York, NY 10025
(212) 874–8282; (800) 2REVIEW
http://www.review.com

*The Dance Directory*
National Dance Association
1900 Association Drive
Reston, VA 20191
(703) 476–3436
http://www.aahperd.org/nda/nda.html

*Dance Magazine College Guide*

*Stern's Performing Arts Directory*

*Dance Magazine*
33 West 60th Street, 10th floor
New York, NY 10023
(212) 245–9050

## Job Resources and Summer Dance Programs

*\*ArtSearch*
Theater Communications Group
355 Lexington Avenue
New York, NY 10017
(212) 697–5230
http://www.tcg.org

Note: * indicates job resources.

*Backstage Publications, Inc.*
1515 Broadway, 14th floor
New York, NY 10036
(212) 764–7300; (800) 437–3183
http://www.backstage.com

*Backstage West*
5050 Wilshire Boulevard, 6th floor
Los Angeles, CA 90036
(213) 525–2356

*/**The Calendar of Audition Dates*
P.O. Box 904
New York, NY 10023
(212) 535–3757
http://www.dancepro.com

*The Dance Directory* (Europe or America)
P.O. Box 904
New York, NY 10023
(212) 535–3757
http://www.dancepro.com

*/**Dance Magazine*
33 West 60th Street, 10th floor
New York, NY 10023
(212) 245–9050
http://www.dancemagazine.com

*/**Stern's Performing Arts Directory*
33 West 60th Street, 10th floor
New York, NY 10023
(212) 245–9050

## Medical Insurance

Dance Professionals Associates
440 East 81st Street, Suite 6G
New York, NY 10028
(212) 535–3757
http://www.dancepro.com

Note: * indicates job resources; ** indicates summer dance programs.

## Medical Services and Clinics

### Worldwide

Dance Professionals Associates
440 East 81st Street, Suite 6G
New York, NY 10028
(212) 535–3757
http://www.dancepro.com (lists health care providers
specializing in dance-related medicine)

### Australia

Dance Medicine Australia
10 Cecil Place
Prahran, Victoria, Australia 3181
61–3–9525–1566

### Canada

The Artists Health Centre Project
c/o Joysanne Sidimus (DTRC)
66 Gerrard Street East, Suite 202
Toronto, Ontario M5B 1G3
(416) 595–5655

Centre for Human Performance and Health Promotion
Sir William Osler Health Institute
565 Sanatorium Road, Suite 205
Hamilton, Ontario L9C 7N4
(905) 574–5444

The Musician's Clinic of Canada (also treats dancers)
340 College Street, Suite 440
Toronto, Ontario M5T 3A9
(416) 966–8742

Pilates Centre of Montreal
4965 Queen Mary Street
Montreal, Quebec H3W 1X4
(514) 735–9506

## Israel

Israel Performing Arts Medical Center
30 ibn Gvirol Street
Tel Aviv 64078, Israel
972-3-609147516

The Israel Physiotherapy Clinic
57 Derech Hebron
IL-93546 Jerusalem
972-2-673-2939

## Netherlands

Medical Center for Dancers and Musicians
Westeinde Ziekenhuis
Postbus 432
NL-2501 CK's Gravenhage (The Hague)
31-70-330-20-42

## United Kingdom

British Performing Arts Medicine Trust
60-62 Clapham Road
London SW9 0JJ, England
44-171-840-5588
http://www.cygnet.co.uk/bpamt

Remedial Dance Physiotherapy Clinic
32 Wimpole Street
London W1M 7AE, England
44-171-580-1650

## United States

*Nationwide*

The Method® developed by Joseph Pilates
(nationwide referral service)
Physicalmind Institute
1807 Second Street, Suite 47
Santa Fe, NM 87505
(505) 988-1990; (800) 505-1990

Pilates Studio® Performing Arts Physical Therapy (nationwide referral service)
2121 Broadway, 2nd floor
New York, NY 10023
(212) 875–0189; (800) 474–5283

*California*

Medical Program for the Performing Arts
Loma Linda University Medical Center
P.O. Box 7119
Loma Linda, CA 92354
(909) 799–6144

Peter F. Ostwald Health Program for Performing Artists
University of California School of Medicine
374 Parnassus Avenue
San Francisco, CA 94143
(415) 476–3452

*Connecticut*

Connecticut Center for Dance Medicine
29 North Main Street, 2nd floor
West Hartford, CT 06107
(860) 561–3960

*Illinois*

Medical Program for Performing Artists
Northwestern Memorial Hospital
Rehabilitation Institute of Chicago
345 East Superior Street, Suite 1116
Chicago, IL 60611
(312) 908-ARTS

*Indiana*

Rebound Sports Medicine (Eastside location)
857 Auto Mall Road, Suite 4
Bloomington, IN 47401
(812) 332–6200

Rebound Sports Medicine (Westside location)
639 South Walker Street, Suite B
Bloomington, IN 47403
(812) 336–9333

*Maryland*

National Rehabilitation Hospital
Suburban Regional Rehab
3 Bethesda Metro Center, Suite 950
Bethesda, MD 20814
(301) 654–9160

Sinai Rehabilitation Center
2401 West Belvedere Avenue
Baltimore, MD 21215
(410) 601–5597

*Massachusetts*

Division of Sports Medicine
Children's Hospital
300 Longwood Avenue
Boston, MA 02115
(617) 355–6028

*Michigan*

Center for Athletic Medicine
6525 Second Avenue, 1st floor
Detroit, MI 48202
(313) 972–4140

*Minnesota*

Fairview Arts Medicine Center
507 Medical Arts Building
825 Nicollet Mall
Minneapolis, MN 55402
(612) 339–9786

*Missouri*

Medical Program for the Performing Arts
Barnes Jewish Hospital
11300 West Pavilion
1 Barnes Jewish Plaza
St. Louis, MO 63110
(314) 454-STAR

Performance Arts Medicine Center
2135 South Fremont Street, 1st floor
Springfield, MO 65804
(417) 888–7989

*Nevada*

Keith Kleven Institute of Orthopaedic, Sports, and Dance
Rehabilitation
3650 South Eastern Avenue, Suite 100
Las Vegas, NV 89109
(702) 731–0831

*New Jersey*

International Foundation for Performing Arts Medicine
55 West Lindsley Road
North Caldwell, NJ 07006
(973) 890–7874

Kessler Institute for Rehabilitation
1199 Pleasant Valley Way
West Orange, NJ 07052
(973) 243–6844

*New York*

Harkness Center for Dance Injuries
Hospital for Joint Diseases
301 East 17th Street
New York, NY 10003
(212) 598–6022

Miller Health Care Institute for Performing Artists
St. Luke's–Roosevelt Hospital
425 West 59th Street, 6th floor
New York, NY 10019
(212) 523–6200


Westside Dance Physical Therapy Center
2109 Broadway, Suite 204
New York, NY 10023
(212) 787–0390


*North Carolina*

Comprehensive Physical Therapy Center
115 Timber Hill Place
Chapel Hill, NC 27514
(919) 967–5959


Duke University Medical Center
Sports Medicine
P.O. Box 3965
Durham, NC 27710
(919) 681–7678


*Ohio*

Clinic for the Performing Arts
Center for Orthopedic Care
2123 Auburn Avenue, Suite 235
Cincinnati, OH 45219
(513) 651–0094


Franciscan Medical Center, Sports Medicine Center
1 Franciscan Way
Dayton, OH 45408
(937) 229–6692

*Pennsylvania*

Center for Sports Medicine
University of Pittsburgh Medical Center
4601 Baum Boulevard, 2nd floor
Pittsburgh, PA 15213
(412) 578–3302

Performing Arts Physical Therapy at Pennsylvania Ballet
1101 South Broad Street
Philadelphia, PA 19147
(215) 551–4694

*Virginia*

Body Dynamics Rehab Services
3808 Wilson Boulevard
Arlington, VA 22203
(703) 779–0905

*Washington*

Capital Hill Physical Therapy
413 Fairview Avenue North
Seattle, WA 98109
(206) 405–3560

Seattle Sports Physical Therapy
501 First Avenue South
Seattle, WA 98104
(206) 467–6705

Virginia Mason Medical Center
1100 Ninth Avenue
Seattle, WA 98111
(206) 223–6885

# Mental Health

American Psychological Association
(800) 259–1991
http://www.apa.org

National Institute of Mental Health
(800) 421–4211

## Nutrition

The Nutrition Hotline
(800) 366–1655

## Résumés and Auditioning

*The Audition Handbook for Ballet*, by Carole Augustus (1997).
c/o Carole Augustus
Schifflaube 38
CH-3011 Bern, Switzerland
41–31–312–12–28

Dance Professionals Associates
440 East 81st Street, Suite 6G
New York, NY 10028
(212) 535–3757
http://www.dancepro.com (lists auditions)

*Your Dance Résumé: A Preparatory Guide to the Audition*,
by Eric Wolfram (1994).
Dancepress
735 Harrison Street
San Francisco, CA 94107
(415) 974–0551

## Unions

Actors' Equity Association
165 West 46th Street, 15th floor
New York, NY 10036
(212) 869–8530

American Guild of Musical Artists
1727 Broadway, 2nd floor
New York, NY 10019
(212) 265–3687

American Guild of Variety Artists
184 Fifth Avenue, 6th floor
New York, NY 10010
(212) 675–1003

Independent Artists of America (not affiliated with the
AFL-CIO; open to ABT dancers and possibly to those with
other dance companies)
c/o Leonard Leibowitz
400 Madison Avenue
New York, NY 10017
(212) 832–8322

Screen Actors Guild
1515 Broadway, 44th floor
New York, NY 10036
(212) 944–1030

# $\mathcal{B}$ibliography

American Psychiatric Association. (1994). *Diagnostic and Statistical Manual of Mental Disorders* (4th ed.). Washington, D.C.: American Psychiatric Association.

Augustus, C. (1997). *The Audition Handbook for Ballet*. Bern, Switzerland: Carole Augustus.

Bakker, F. C. (1988). "Personality Differences Between Young Dancers and Non-Dancers." *Personality and Individual Differences*, 9, 121–131.

Brukner, P., and Khan, K. (1993). *Clinical Sports Medicine*. Sydney, Australia: McGraw-Hill.

Dweck, C. S. (1995, Sept.). "Students' Theories About Their Intelligence: Implications for the Gifted." Paper presented at the Fifth Annual Esther Katz Rosen Symposium on the Psychological Development of Gifted Children, Lawrence, Kans.

Freudenberger, H. J., and Richelson, G. (1980). *Burn-Out: The High Cost of High Achievement*. New York: Anchor/Doubleday, p. 17.

Gardner, H. (1993). *Multiple Intelligences: The Theory in Practice*. New York: Basic Books.

Gardner, H. (in press). "Are There Additional Intelligences? The Case for Naturalist, Spiritual, and Existential Intelligences." In J. Kane (Ed.), *Education, Information, and Transformation*. Upper Saddle River, N.J.: Prentice Hall.

Gauron, E. F. (1984). *Mental Training for Peak Performance*. Lansing, N.Y.: Sport Science Associates.

Hamilton, L. H. (1996, Nov.). "Dancers' Health Survey, Part I: To Your Health." *Dance Magazine*, 56–60.

Hamilton, L. H. (1997, Feb.). "Dancers' Health Survey, Part II: From Injury to Peak Performance." *Dance Magazine*, 60–65.

Hamilton, L. H. (1997). *The Person Behind the Mask: A Guide to Performing Arts Psychology*. Greenwich, Conn.: Ablex.

Hamilton, L. H., and Hamilton, W. G. (1994). "Occupational Stress in Classical Ballet: The Impact in Different Cultures." *Medical Problems of Performing Artists*, 9, 35–38.

Hamilton, L. H., Hamilton, W. G., Warren, M. P., Keller, K., and Molnar, M. (1997). "Factors Contributing to the Attrition Rate in Elite Ballet Students." *Journal of Dance Medicine and Science*, 1, 131–138.

Hamilton, L. H., Kella, J. J., and Hamilton, W. G. (1995). "Personality and Occupational Stress in Elite Performers." *Medical Problems of Performing Artists*, 10, 86–89.

Lowman, R. L. (1991). *The Clinical Practice of Career Assessment: Interests, Abilities, and Personality*. Washington, D.C.: American Psychological Association.

Martens, R. (1987). *Coaches' Guide to Sport Psychology*. Champaign, Ill.: Human Kinetics.

Nagel, J. J. (1990). "Performance Anxiety and the Performing Musician: A Fear of Failure or a Fear of Success?" *Medical Problems of Performing Artists*, 5, 37–40.

Nicholas, J. A. (1975). "Risk Factors, Sports Medicine and the Orthopedic System: An Overview." *Journal of Sports Medicine*, 3, 243–259.

Robson, B. E., and Gitev, M. (1991). "In Search of Perfection." *Medical Problems of Performing Artists*, 6, 15–20.

Ryan, A. J., and Stephens, R. E. (Eds.). (1987). *Dance Medicine: A Comprehensive Guide*. Chicago: Pluribus Press.

Sargent, D. W. (1963). Weight-Height Relationship of Young Men and Women. *American Journal of Clinical Nutrition*, 13, 318–325.

Steinmetz, J., Brown, L., Hall, D., and Miller, G. (1980). *Managing Stress Before It Manages You*. Palo Alto, Calif.: Bull.

Taylor, J., and Taylor, C. (1995). *Psychology of Dance*. Champaign, Ill.: Human Kinetics.

Tomlinson-Keasey, C., and Little, T. D. (1990). "Predicting Educational Attainment, Occupational Achievement, Intellectual Skill, and Personal Adjustment Among Gifted Men and Women." *Journal of Educational Psychology*, 82, 442–455.

Van Raalte, J. L., and Brewer, B. W. (Eds.). (1996). *Exploring Sport and Exercise Psychology*. Washington, D.C.: American Psychological Association.

Williams, J. M., and Leffingwell, T. R. (1996). "Cognitive Strategies in Sport and Exercise Psychology." In J. L. Van Raalte and B. W. Brewer (Eds.), *Exploring Sport and Exercise Psychology*. Washington, D. C.: American Psychological Association.

Wolfram, E. (1994). *Your Dance Résumé: A Preparatory Guide to the Audition*. San Francisco: Dancepress.

# Further Reading

Barringer, J., and Schlesinger, S. (1997). *The Pointe Book, Revised: Shoes, Training, and Technique.* Princeton, N.J.: Princeton Book Company.

Berardi, G. (1991). *Finding Balance: Fitness and Training for a Lifetime in Dance.* Princeton, N.J.: Princeton Book Company.

Bolles, R. N. (1997). *What Color Is Your Parachute?* Berkeley, Calif.: Ten Speed Press.

Garwood, A., and Melnick, B. (1995). *What Everyone Can Do to Fight AIDS.* San Francisco: Jossey-Bass.

Grant, G. (1983). *Technical Manual and Dictionary of Classical Ballet* (rev. 3rd ed.). New York: Dover.

Hamilton, L. H., and Stricker, G. (1989). "Balanchine's Children." *Medical Problems of Performing Artists, 4,* 143–147.

Neale, W. (1982). *Ballet Life Behind the Scenes.* New York: Crown.

Ryan, A. J., and Stephens, R. E. (1988). *The Dancer's Complete Guide to Healthcare and a Long Career.* Chicago: Bonus Books.

Shoop, R. L., and Edwards, D. L. (1994). *How to Stop Sexual Harassment in Our Schools: A Handbook and Curriculum Guide for Administrators and Teachers.* Needham Heights, Mass.: Allyn & Bacon.

Sidimus, J. (1987). *Exchanges: Life After Dance.* Toronto: Press of Terpsichore Limited.

Vincent, L. M. (1989). *Competing with the Sylph: The Quest for the Perfect Dance Body* (2nd ed.). Princeton, N.J.: Princeton Book Company.

# About the Author

Linda H. Hamilton, Ph.D., is a clinical psychologist who previously danced with the New York City Ballet. Her private practice is concerned with the emotional stresses around performance. She is also a regular consultant at the School of American Ballet and the Alvin Ailey American Dance Center; the author of numerous professional papers on the topics of eating disorders, stage fright, and career transition; and the monthly advice columnist for *Dance Magazine*. Hamilton is listed in the *Marquis Who's Who of American Women*, and her work with performers is featured in a documentary film called *A Vision to Heal*. Her first book, *The Person Behind the Mask: A Guide to Performing Arts Psychology* (1997, Ablex Publishing Corp.), is the first of its kind in the new field of performance psychology to address emotional problems among entertainers.

# Index

**A**

Abusive directors, 120–121
Abusive teachers/teaching, 1, 5, 13–14, 41–47; assessment of, 50–51; performance anxiety caused by, 42, 45, 124–125; prevalence of, 42; and self esteem, 46–47; sexual harassment by, 88–89, 90–91; verbal attacks by, 42–44; working when injured and, 44–46. *See also* Sexual harassment; Teachers
Academic achievement, 38
Achilles tendinitis, 163
Actors' Equity Association, 120, 211
Actor's Fund of America, 170, 193
Adolescence, 5; sexual orientation and, 86–87
Aerobic exercise, 68, 69, 155
Age: of beginning training, 12–13, 18–19, 56, 153; and injury potential, 153; older, 180–181; of retiring, 26; and substance abuse, 134, 135
Agents, 116–117; resources for, 117, 193
Aging, 180–181
AIDS/HIV infection, 6, 168–170; prevalence of, 166; resources for, 170, 193–194; risk factors for, 168–169; support for, 169–170; treatment of, 169–170
Alcohol use/abuse: prevalence of, 134, 165; treatment of, 135–136
Alcoholics Anonymous, 135–136
Alvin Ailey American Dance Center, 3, 100; on-site child care of, 84
Amateurs, driven, 19
Amenorrhea, 61, 64, 70, 71
American Ballet Theatre (ABT), 13–14, 115; injuries at, 147, 154; injury prevention at, 149; union of, 120

American College of Sports Medicine, 195
American Council on Exercise, 196
American Dance Therapy Association, 185, 196
American Dietetic Association, 72
American Guild of Musical Artists (AGMA), 120, 121, 211
American Guild of Variety Artists, 212
American Physical Therapy Association, 186, 196
American Psychiatric Association, 58, 132
American Psychological Association, 210
Amphetamines, 134, 135
Anatomy: of dancers, 15–16; and injuries, 15, 17, 23, 147–148, 151–153; of musculoskeletal system, 151–153; problems in, 16–17. *See also* Body shape; Weight
Anderson, B., 200
Angelic Support Bra, 74, 194
Anorexia nervosa, 58, 62, 64–65; diagnostic criteria for, 64; menstrual problems of, 61, 64, 71; types of, 64. *See also* Eating disorders
Anxiety: mental, 129–130, 140–141; physical, 130–131, 142–145. *See also* Performance anxiety
Apparel, resources for, 194
Apprenticeship, 115
Arousal regulation, 142–145
ArtsCare catalogue, 194
*ArtSearch*, 186, 202
Astaire, F., 31
Asthma, 165, 166–167
Attitude, 177–178
*Audition Handbook for Ballet* (Augustus), 211

Audition package, 6; cover letter in, 107, 109; dance résumé in, 105–107, 108; photographs in, 107, 109–110; purpose of, 104–105; resources for, 211; videotapes in, 110–111

Audition phone calls, 111–112

Auditions, 113–115; agents for, 116–117; ballet, 114; modern dance, 114; musical theater, 114; resources for, 114, 211. *See also* Performance anxiety; Performance enhancement

Augustus, C., 211

Australia, medical services in, 204

Australian Ballet School, 21

**B**

*Backstage*, 109, 114, 120

*Backstage Publications, Inc.*, 203

*Backstage West*, 203

Balanchine, G., 2, 24, 39, 83

*Balanchine Essays, The*, 201

Balanchine style, 24, 116

Ballet, classical, 23–25, 32; auditions for, 114; physical challenges of, compared to sports, 80; styles of, 24–25; styles of, and injuries, 154

Ballet, modern, 26

Ballet dancers: anatomy of, 147–148; body shape of, 23, 25; weight of, 23, 58, 59

Ballet training: age and, 12, 153–154; anatomy and, 15–17, 23; ballet styles and, 23–25; college and, 49; dropouts of, 16–17; injuries of, 153; injury prevention in, 162–163; professional schools for, 113; unrealistic expectations in, 20–21. *See also* Dance training

Ballistic stretching, 163

Ballroom dancing, 26–28; international style of, 27; Latin American, 27; weight and, 28

Barbiturates, 134, 135

*Barre*, 162–163

Barringer, J., 200

Baryshnikov, M., 26, 80, 97

Bennett, M., 30

Benzoin tincture, 151

Betts, I., 169–170

*Bible of Performing Arts Education, The* (Topaz), 201

Binge-eating disorder, 62–63, 66–67

Binge-eating/purging anorexic, 64. *See also* Anorexia nervosa

Bissell, P., 135

Blasis, C., 23

Blisters, 151

Body image, 5; and basic anatomy, 15–16; of dancers, 58; of girls, 58; and sexual harassment, 91

Body shape, 5, 55–60; of ballet dancers, 23, 25; changes in, 56; effects of dance training on, 56; of modern dancers, 25; of young dancers, 55–56. *See also* Anatomy; Fat; Weight

Books, dance, 199–200

Boston Ballet, 24

Boston Ballet II, 115

Bouncing, 163

Bras, 74; resources for, 194

Breakin' (break dancing), 28–29

Breast size, 74

*Bring in 'da Noise, Bring in 'da Funk*, 31

Broadway Dance Center, 29

Brooks, V., 110

Buck-and-wing, 31

Bulimia nervosa, 62, 65–66; diagnostic criteria for, 65–66; nonpurging type of, 66; purging type of, 66; types of, 66

Bunheads, Inc., 194

Bunions, 150

Burnout, 174; prevention of, 176; symptoms of, 175–176

*Burn-Out: The High Cost of Achievement* (Freudenberger and Pichelson), 175–176

Business, starting a, 184–185

**C**

Caffeine, 71

Calcium intake, 70–71, 156

*Calendar of Audition Dates*, 114, 203

California: career transition center in, 195; medical services and clinics in, 206

Calling, sense of, 10–11

Calorie intake, 70–72, 73, 155

Canada: career transition center in, 194; medical services and clinics in, 204

Carbohydrates, 69–70, 73

Career advice, dance. *See* Professional career development

Career transition centers, 6; resources for, 194–195

Career Transitions for Dancers (CTFD), 187, 195

CareerLine (National Career Transition for Dancers) hotline, 195

Careers, postdance: early preparation for, 182–184; emotional recovery and, 191; obstacles to, 187–188; options for,

185–187; resources for, 194–195; starting a business for, 184–185
Cattle call, 109
Cecchetti, E., 24
Cecchetti method, 24
Cellulite, 73–74
Center for Menopause, Hormonal Disorders, and Women's Health, 71
Centers for Disease Control (CDC), 170; hotline, 193
Champion, G., 30
Charleston, 30
Child care, 84
Chmelar, R. D., 200
Choreography, 183–184
Chorus Line, A, 30
Christine Valmy International School, 195
Cigarette smoking, 165
Clarkson, P., 200
Classical ballet. See Ballet, classical; Ballet training
Coach Effectiveness Training (CET), 53
Cognitive anxiety management, 140–141. See also Faulty beliefs; Self-talk
"Cognitive Strategies in Sport and Exercise Psychology," 142
College: before dance career, 101; for career transition, 186
College dance programs, 49, 50; resources for, 202
Comparisons, inappropriate, 51, 78; and performance anxiety, 128
Competition: in dance schools, 48–50; among dance students, 5, 51, 77–79; and performance anxiety, 123, 128; strategies for dealing with, 79
Competitions: applying for, 117–118; ballroom dance, 27, 28; hip-hop, 29; resources for, 118, 197–198
Complaint, sexual harassment, 94
Compulsive behaviors, 95
Connecticut, medical center in, 206
Controlled imagery, 139
Cornish College of the Arts, 50
Corrections, constant, 52
Cosmetic surgery, 74
Cover letters, 107, 109
Crenshaw, D., 105, 107
Crisis intervention, for sexual harassment, 94–95
Cross-gender behavior, 86–87
Cruise ship performing, 120
Cunningham, M., 26

**D**

Dance community: changes in, 3–4; relationships within, 77–79, 188; retirement from, 188
Dance companies: abuse in, 120–121; agents and, 117; career advancement in, 118–119; checking out, 115–116; directories of, 115; postdance careers with, 186; salaries of, 119; starting with small, 177; unions and, 119–121
Dance Companies Resettlement Fund and Dancers Trust, 195
Dance Directory, The, 115, 203
Dance Educators of America, 198
Dance Europe, 201
Dance floors, 149
Dance Magazine: advice column, 2, 4, 7, 113; audition ads, 114; contact information, 194, 201, 202, 203
Dance Magazine College Guide, 49, 202
Dance Magazine survey results: on abusive teaching, 42; on academic achievement, 38; on body image, 58; on health problems, 165–166; on injuries, 148, 153; on performance anxiety, 129; on sexual harassment, 91–93; on sexual orientation, 85–86; on substance use, 134–135; on weight and height, 58–59
Dance Masters of America, 198
Dance medicine: emergence of, 3–4; resources for, 164–165, 195–197, 204–210
Dance Medicine and Science Bibliography, 199
Dance Medicine Resource Guide (Hagins), 199
Dance On Foundation, 186
Dance organizations, 4, 198–199
Dance Professionals Associates, 4, 104, 170, 203, 204, 211
Dance publications, 199–201
Dance schools: ballroom dance, 28; eating disorders education in, 60, 67; establishment of, 184–185; hip-hop, 29; level of competition in, 48–50; nutrition education in, 60; possessiveness of, 36–38; professional, 112–113; safety in, 50–51; selection of, 13–14, 47–51, 112–113; sexual harassment in, 90–94, 96. See also Dance training; Teachers; Teaching practices
Dance techniques, 4, 22–32; and injuries, of, 152, 153–154; prevalence of, by type, 23; selection of, 22–32, 152; and school possessiveness, 37; types of, 23–32. See

*also* Ballet *headings*; Ballroom dancing; Hip-Hop; Jazz dance; Modern dance; Tap dance
Dance therapist career, 185; resources for, 196–197
Dance training, 4, 5, 12–13; age of beginning, 12–13, 18–19, 56, 153; benefits of good, 36–41; college and, 49; discipline and, 36–38; effects of, on body shape and size, 56; feedback in, 40–41; injuries in, 153–155; late, 12–13, 18–19; over-training syndrome in, 179–180; work habits and, 38–40. *See also* Ballet training; Teachers; Teaching practices
Dancer Transition Resource Centre, 194
Dancers, 1–4; anatomy of, 15–16; expectations of, assessment of, 18–22; factors in creation of, 4, 9–17, 33; health of, 165–171; injuries of, 147–149; kinesthetic intelligence in, 11–12; older, 180–181; passion of, 10–11; personality and temperament of, 14–15; supply and demand for, 112. *See also* Female dancers; Male dancers; Professional dancers; Student dancers
Dancers Over 40, Inc., 4, 181, 198
*Dance/USA*, 166
Dancing: to lose weight, 57–58; passion for, 10–11; as way of life, 1, 2, 173–174
*Dancing Longer, Dancing Stronger* (Watkins and Clarkson), 200
Dating, 82–85; and late puberty, 82; obstacles to, 82–85; in same dance company, 84–85; teachers' and directors' disapproval of, 83–84
de Mille, A., 30
*Demi-pointe*, training in, 20, 21
Depression, 167–168; and eating disorders, 63–64; and injuries, 158; prevalence of, 165, 166, 167; symptoms of, 168; treatment of, 168
Designer drugs, 134, 135
Diet: healthy, 69–72; and injuries, 155–156; resources for, 72, 213
*Diet for Dancers* (Chmelar and Fitt), 200
Dieting, 5, 57; healthy approaches to, 69–75; problems of, 61–62. *See also* Weight
Directories: of agents, 117; company, 115–116
Directors: abusive, 120–121; addressing cover letters to, 107, 109; disapproval of, of dancers' intimate relationships, 83–84
Discipline, 36–38

Discrimination complaints, 94, 121
Doug Elkin Dance Company, 29
Dove, U., 170
Dropouts/dropping out: aging and, 180–181; avoiding, 173–181; burnout and, 174–176; injuries and, 17, 178–180; problems of, 16–17; unemployment and, 176–178. *See also* Retirement; Transitions
Drug dependence, 134, 135–136. *See also* Substance use/abuse
Drug tolerance, 134. *See also* Substance use/abuse
Dubé, A., 121
Dulaine, P., 28
Duncan, I., 26
Dweck, C. S., 39

**E**
Eating: healthy, 69–72; and injuries, 160
Eating disorders, 5, 62–67; attitudes and, 63; conditions for developing, 63–64; and dance school education, 60; and dropouts, 17; overcoming, 67–75; prevalence of, 6, 64, 165, 166; resources for, 67, 201; sexual harassment and, 91; types of, 62–63, 64–67; and weight loss, 61
Edwards, D. L., 96
Effort, 39–40
Elastikon, 151
Emotional problems: abusive teaching and, 42–43; from dieting, 62; of injuries, 158, 160–161, 162; performance and, 6; of retirement, 187–191; resources for, 210–211; working with injuries and, 45. *See also* Depression; Eating disorders; Performance anxiety
Employment, dance: agents for, 116–117; auditions for, 113–115; company directories for, 115–116; dance school selection and, 112–113; prevalence of full-time, 6, 23; resources for, 114, 202–203; strategies for finding, 112–121, 176–178. *See also* Careers, postdance; Job opportunities; Professional career development; Survival jobs
Endurance training, 69
Entity theory, 39
Environmental factors, in injuries, 149–151
Epsom salts, 151
Equal Rights Act of 1964, 96
Estrogen, and dieting, 61
Estrogen-replacement therapy, 71

European dance company auditions, 114
Exercise programs, 15; discipline and, 37;
    for hip-hop, 29; for injury prevention,
    154–155; for older dancers, 181; for
    weight control, 68–69, 73, 74–75
Expectations, realistic versus unrealistic,
    18–22
Extrinsic asthma, 166
Extroverts, 101–102

**F**

Fabulon, 150
Family planning, 103
Fat, in specific body parts, 73–74. *See also*
    Weight
Fat intake, 70–72, 73
Faulty beliefs: abusive teaching and,
    46–47; cognitive anxiety management
    for, 140–141; mental anxiety and,
    129–130
Fear. *See* Performance anxiety; Stage fright
Feedback: negative, 50–51; positive use of,
    40–41
Feldenkrais Guild, 196
Female dancers: age of training of, 12;
    health problems of, 165, 166; injuries of,
    153; of modern dance, 25; nutritional
    needs of, 70–71, 156; pregnancy and,
    103; pubertal changes of, 56; sexual
    harassment of, 91, 92, 93; substance
    abuse of, 134–135; survival jobs and,
    102–103; and weight, 58
Fitt, S., 200
Flashbacks, 95
Fletcher, H., 38
Flexibility: basic anatomy and, 17; for
    injury prevention, 154
Florida State University, 50
Flow, achieving state of, 145–146
Foot problems, 149–151, 153–154
Footware resources, 194. *See also Pointe*
    shoes; Toe shoes
Fourteenth Amendment to the Constitu-
    tion of the United States, 96
Fox-trot, 30
Free style hip-hop, 29
Freudenberger, H. J., 175–176
Frozen fright, 89, 95
Fugate, J., 117
Full Circle Productions, 29
Fusion dance, 26

**G**

Gardner, H., 11
Garwood, A., 170, 200

Gauron, E. F., 129
Genes: and anatomy, 152; and weight,
    56–57, 67. *See also* Anatomy
GhettOriginal, 29
Glover, S., 31
Glycogen, 69
Goal setting: for imagery training, 139; for
    injury recovery, 159–160; for perfor-
    mance enhancement, 136–137
Godunov, A., 135
Graham, M., 26
Graham contraction, 90
Graham technique, training in, 49–50
*Grands pliés,* 162–163
Gray, D., 90
Grief stages, 188–189. *See also* Loss;
    Mourning
Grievance filing, 121

**H**

Hagins, M., 199
Hamburg, J., 90
Hamilton, L. H., 2–3
Hamilton, W. G., 154
Harvey, C., 59
Health: and eating, 69–72; of older
    dancers, 180–181; status of dancers',
    165–166; and weight control, 61–62,
    68–75
Health care products, resources for, 194
Health insurance, 104, 170–171; resources
    for, 170–171, 203
Health problems, 6, 165–171; abusive
    teaching and, 42–43, 45; resources for,
    206–213. *See also* AIDS; Asthma;
    Depression; Eating disorders; Injuries
Healthier Dancer Programme, 53
Height, and weight, 59–60
*Hello, Dolly!,* 30
High school dance programs, 202
Hinkle, S., 105, 107
Hip-hop, 28–29; styles of, 28–29
HIV infection. *See* AIDS/HIV infection
Hobbies, 81
Homosexuality, 85–87
Humiliation, 89
Humphrey, D., 26
Hypermobility, 148

**I**

Illinois, medical services in, 206
Imagery training, 137–140
Impatience, teacher, 50
Imperial Ballet School, 24
Incremental theory, 39

Independent Artists of America, 120, 212
Indiana, medical services and clinics in, 206
Inhalers, asthma, 167
Injuries, 6, 147–165; abusive teaching and, 42–46, 51; acute care for, 164–165; anatomical factors in, 15, 17, 23, 147–148, 151–153; auditioning with, 113; coping mechanisms for, 158–162; diagnosis of, 157–158; dietary factors in, 155–156; dropouts and, 17, 178–180; environmental factors in, 149–151; of feet, 149–151; musculoskeletal system and, 151–153; paying attention to, 164–165; prevalence of, 147–149; prevention of, 152–153, 162–165, 179–180; professional help for, 157–158, 164; psychological impact of, 158; psychological pressures and, 156–157; realistic goals for, 159–160; risk of, 147–148; steps, style, and technique factors in, 153–155; subtle, 181; treatment of, 157–162; working in spite of, 44–46, 51, 156–157
Inspiration, teacher, 50–51
Intensity, of physiological arousal, 142–145
International Association for Dance Medicine and Science, 4, 135, 199
International Ballet Association Luxembourg, 197
International Ballet Competition, 197
International Ballet Competition Maya, 197
International Competition Alicia Alonso, 197
International Conference of Symphony and Opera Musicians, 129
International Organization for the Transition of Professional Dancers, 187, 199
Intimate relationships. See Dating; Relationships
Intrinsic asthma, 166
Introduction to Dance Medicine: Keeping Dancers Dancing, 201
Introverts, 101–102
Intrusive thoughts, 95
Israel, medical services and clinics in, 205

J

Jaffe, S., 59
Jazz dance, 30–31; weight and, 31
Jealousy, of nondancers, 5. See also Relationships
Jitterbug, 30
Job opportunities, 112; auditions for, 113–115; ballroom dance, 28; company directories for, 115–116; hip-hop, 29; jazz dance, 31; resources for, 114, 196–197, 204–205; for survival jobs, 103–104; taking advantage of, 118–119; tap dance, 32. See also Employment; Professional career development; Survival jobs
Journal, for recording sexual harassment, 94
Journal of Dance Medicine and Science, 200
Juilliard School, 28, 38
Junk food, 72

K

Kelly, G., 31
Khan, K., 21
Kinesthetic intelligence, 4, 11–12
Kistler, D., 97
Koch, P., 70
Kübler-Ross, E., 187
Kung fu, 29

L

Latin American dances, 27
Lee, B., 29
Leffingwell, T. R., 142
Line, 23
Liposuction, 74
Lockin', 29
Lopez, L., 84
Loss, at retirement, 187–191; coping with, 189; grief stages and, 188–189; letting go of dance and, 190; recovery from, 190–191
Lower Extermity Dance Medicine: Orthopedic Examination with Dr. William Hamilton, 201
LSD, 134, 135
Luigi, 30
Lunging, 163

M

Macaluso, S., 164–165
Magazines, dance, 201
Makarova, N., 59
Makeup artist career resource, 195
Male dancers: age of training of, 12; calorie and fat intake for, 70; health problems of, 165–166; injuries of, 153; of modern dance, 25; nutritional needs of, 70, 156; pubertal changes of, 56; sexual harassment of, 91, 92; sexual orientation of, 86–87; substance abuse of, 134–135; teasing of, 80
Marceau, Y., 28
Marijuana, 134, 135
Martens, R., 138–139

Martha Graham Dance Company, 49–50, 106, 131
Martha Graham School of Contemporary Dance, 49–50, 90
Martial arts, 29
Martins, P., 84, 97
Maryland, medical services and clinics in, 207
Massachusetts, medical center in, 207
Meadows School of the Arts, 50
Medical services and clinics, 204–210
Melnick, B., 170, 200
Men. See Male dancers
Menstrual problems, 5; and calcium intake, 70; and dieting, 61, 71; and estrogen replacement therapy, 71
Mental anxiety, 129–130; reduction of, 130, 140–141. See also Performance anxiety; Performance enhancement
Mental health resources, 210–211
Mental skills training: for career transition, 191; for injury recovery, 160–161; for performance enhancement, 137–142. See also Performance enhancement
Merce Cunningham Company, 103
Metropolitan Life Insurance Company weight tables, 59
Miami City Ballet, 24
Michigan, medical center in, 207
Minelli, L., 97
Minnesota, medical center in, 207
Missouri, medical services and clinics in, 208
Modern dance, 25–26; auditions for, 114; body shape and, 25; professional training for, 113
Mood disorders. See Depression
Mourning, at retirement, 187–191; letting go of dance and, 190; process of, 188–189; recovery and, 190–191; responses to loss and, 189
Multiple Intelligences (Gardner), 11
Muscle Fitness Book, The 163
Musculoskeletal system: and aging, 180; and injuries, 151–153; and stretching, 163. See also Anatomy; Body shape; Injuries
Musical theater, 30, 31, 113; agents for, 116–117; auditions for, 114

N

Nagel, J. J., 13
Narcotics Anonymous, 135–136
National AIDS Information Clearing House, 193
National Dance Association, 199

National Dance Council of America, 199
National Health and Social Life Survey, 87
National Institute of Mental Health, 168, 211
Negative self-talk, 129–130; overcoming, 141–142
Negative thoughts, abusive teaching and, 46–47
Netherlands: career transition center in, 194; medical center in, 205
Nevada, medical center in, 208
New Jersey, medical services and clinics in, 208
New York: career transition center in, 195; medical services and clinics in, 208
New York City Ballet, 2, 83, 84, 97, 117; apprenticeship at, 115; bras used by, 74; feedback in, 40; Hamilton at, 39, 49, 118, 186; injuries at, 147, 154; salaries at, 119; training internships at, for non-dance positions, 186; union of, 119–120
New York State Coalition Against Sexual Assault, 90
New York State Theater, 137
Nicholas, J. A., 80
Nightmares, 95
North American Society of Teachers of the Alexander Technique, 196
North Carolina, medical services and clinics in, 209
North Carolina School of the Arts (NCSA), 88, 89, 94
Nutrition, 60, 69–72; and injuries, 155–156, 160; resources for, 72, 211
Nutrition Hotline, 72, 211

O

Ohio, medical services and clinics in, 209
Oklahoma!, 30
Older dancers, 180–181
Olichney, J., 167, 168
Olympic athletes, performance enhancement techniques of, 136, 141. See also Performance enhancement
Olympics, ballroom dancing in, 28
Open calls, 109; finding out about, 114
Organizations, dance, 4, 198–199
Outside interests, 81, 100
Overachievers, 156
Overeaters Anonymous, 201
Overtraining syndrome, 179–180

P

Pain relievers, 164
Parental support, 13

Paris International Dance Competition, 117–118

Partner dancing, 27–28

*Passé*, training in, 21

Passion, 10–11

Peak flow meter, 167

Pennsylvania, medical services and clinics in, 210

Perfectionism: performance anxiety and, 127–128; temperament and, 14–15

Performance anxiety, 6; abusive teaching and, 42, 45, 124–125; competitive feelings and, 128; inadequate stage experience and, 125–126; mental anxiety and, 129–130; perfectionism and, 127–128; physical anxiety and, 130–131; self-medication of, 133–136; social phobia and, 132–133; sources of, 123–128; stage fright and, 131–133; strategies for reducing, 136–146; symptoms of, 129–136

Performance enhancement, 6, 136–146; cognitive anxiety management for, 140–141; goal setting for, 136–137; imagery training for, 137–140; physiological arousal regulation for, 142–145; self-talk for, 141–142; temperament and, 15

Performing Arts Medicine Association, 4

Personal inventory: for postdance career, 182; for survival jobs, 100–102

Personality: of dancers, 14–15; and survival jobs, 101–102

Photographs, for auditions, 107, 109–110

Physical anxiety, 130–131; reduction of, 131, 142–145. *See also* Performance anxiety

Physical therapist career, 185–186; resources for, 195–197

Physicalmind Institute, 196

Pilates Centre of Montreal, 204

Pilates method, 15, 37, 68–69; for injury prevention, 154–155; in injury rehabilitation, 161; resources for, 196

Pilates Studio, 197

Pilates trainer career, 100

Placement, 154

*Pointe*: age of training in, 20, 21, 153–154; basic anatomy and, 17; unrealistic expectations of, 20, 21

*Pointe Book, Revised,* 200

*Pointe Book, The,* 154

*Pointe* shoes, 149–151

Poppin', 29

Posttraumatic stress disorder, 95–96

Prevention of injury, 152–153, 162–165, 179–180; listening to your body for, 164–165; stretching for, 163; warm-ups for, 162–163

Prix de Lausanne, 198

Professional career development: agents for, 116–117; aspirations for, 5–6, 99–121; audition package for, 104–112; auditions for, 113–115; competitions and, 117–118; dance company jobs and, 118–119; dance company selection for, 115–116; dance school selection and, 112–113; finding dance jobs for, 112–118, 176–178; resources for, 204–205; survival jobs and, 99–104, 121; unions and, 119–121. *See also* Audition package; Employment; Job opportunities

Professional Children's School, 82

Professional dancers: depression of, 167; injuries of, 148–149

Progressive muscle relaxation, 144–145

Protein, 70, 71

*Psychology of Dance* (Taylor and Taylor), 143–145

Psychotherapy, 2–3, 168, 192

Puberty, 56, 82

Publications, dance, 199–201

**R**

Rape, 94

Rape crisis centers, 94–95

Rehabilitation: coping mechanisms for, 158–162; resources for, 204–210

Relationships, 5, 77–97; competition among dancers and, 5, 51, 77–79; creating, 96–97; in the dance community, 5, 77–79; dating obstacles and, 82–85; models for, 97; with nondancers, 5, 78, 79–81; scheduling demands and, 81, 85; sexual orientation and, 85–87; touring and, 85. *See also* Dating

Relaxation exercises, 144–145

*Relevé* position, basic anatomy and, 17

Renfrew Center, 67, 201

Restricting anorexic, 64. *See also* Anorexia nervosa

Résumés, dance, 105–107; chronological, 106–107; format for, 106–107; functional, 107; information to include in, 106; outline for, 108; references in, 106; resources for, 211. *See also* Audition package

Retirement, 6; ages of, 26; avoiding premature, 173–181; loss and mourning in, 187–191; preparation for, 182–184; reasons for, 181. *See also* Careers, postdance; Dropouts/dropping out; Transitions

RICE (rest, ice, compression, and elevation), 164
Richelson, G., 175–176
Robbins, J., 30
Rockettes, 32
*Ross Reports Television and Film*, 117, 193
Rosselini, I., 97
Royal Academy of Dance (RAD), 24; certification, 106
Russian Imperial School, 24

**S**

Safety, classroom, 50–51
St. Denis, R., 26
Salaries, 119
Same-sex preference, 85–87
Sargent's weight-height table, 59, 60
*Saturday Night Fever*, 27
Scheduling demands, and relationships, 81, 85
Schlesinger, S., 200
School of American Ballet (SAB), 14, 68, 97, 115, 167; age of *pointe* training in, 153–154; ballroom dance training at, 28; dropouts of, 16; Hamilton at, 2, 3, 35; injuries at, 147–148; nutritionist at, 70; *pointe* training in, 20; résumé support at, 105, 107, 108; video auditions for, 110
Screen Actors Guild, 120, 212
Self-esteem, abusive teaching and, 46–47, 50–51
Self-medication: for anxiety control, 133–136; for injuries, 164
Self-sabotage: abusive teaching and, 42–43, 124–125; temperament and, 14–15; working with injuries and, 45
Self-talk: negative, 129–130; for performance enhancement, 141–142; recording, 141–142
Sensory awareness, 138–139
Sexual harassment, 1, 5, 88–96; versus consensual sexual relations, 89; in dance schools, 90–94, 96; gender and, 91–93; nature of, 88–90; power and, 88–89; prevalence of, 90–94; reactions to, 89, 91, 94–96; recovery from, 95–96; strategies for stopping, 93–94; trauma of, 94–96
Sexual harassment policies, 96
Sexual orientation, 85–87
Sexual relationships. *See* Dating; Relationships
Sexually transmitted diseases (STDs), 169; prevalence of, 166. *See also* AIDS/HIV infection
Shoop, R. L., 96

Silence: about AIDS, 169–170; about dancers' problems, 1–2
Social phobia, 132–133
Socializing, 5; dating and, 82–85; and dedication, 173–174; scheduling demands and, 81. *See also* Dating; Relationships
Soft shoe, 31
Southern Methodist University, 50
Spondylolithesis, 17
Sports drinks, 155
Sprains, 157–158
Stage experience, 125–126
Stage fright: behavioral signs of, 131–132; diagnosis of, 132–133; due to abusive teaching, 42, 45, 124–125; due to anxiety, 123. *See also* Performance anxiety
Stamina, 154
*Stern's Performing Arts Directory*, 116, 117, 193, 194, 202, 203
Strength, 154
Stress fractures, 5; and amenorrhea, 71; and dieting, 61
Stretch box, 163
Stretching, 163
*Stretching* (Anderson), 200
Student dancers: competition among, 5, 51, 77–79; injuries of, 147–148
Substance use/abuse, 133–136; prevalence of, 134–135, 165; resources for, 135–136; treatment of, 135–136
Sugar, 155
Summer dance programs, 202–203
Summer Olympics, 167
Support groups: for substance addiction, 135–136; for weight control, 74, 201–202
Survival jobs, 6, 99–104, 121; examples of, 103–104; personal inventory for, 100–102; resources for, 102, 196–197; selection of, 103–104; women in, 102–103
Swedish Institute, 197

**T**

Talents, 11–12, 33
Tap dance, 31–32; weight and, 32
Taylor, C., 143
Taylor, J., 143
Taylor, P., 26
Teachers: assessment of, 50–51; disapproval of dancers' intimate relationships, 83–84; and eating disorders, 67–68; feedback from, 40–41; inspiring, 52–53; selection of, 13–14; standards for, 53. *See also* Abusive teachers; Dance schools; Dance training

Teaching practices, 35–53; abusive, 1, 5, 13–14, 41–47, 124–125; discipline and, 36–38; effects of, on performance, 124–125; of feedback, 40–41; good, 36–41; inspiring, 52–53; safe, 50–51; sexual harassment and, 90; standards for, 53; work habits and, 38–40. *See also* Abusive teachers/teaching; Dance schools; Dance training

Teasing, from nondancers, 5, 79–81; examples of, 79–81; strategies for dealing with, 80–81

*Technical Manual and Dictionary of Classical Ballet*, 25

Temperament: of dancers, 14–15; and survival jobs, 101–102

Tharp, T., 26, 124

*Tharp!*, 124

Theater dance, 30–31. *See* Musical theater

Theater Instituut Nederland, 194

Time out, 179

Toe shoes, 21, 149–151

Topaz, M., 203

Touring, and relationships, 85

Training. *See* Dance training

Transitions, 182–187; career, 6, 182–187, 190–191; mourning retirement losses and, 187–191; obstacles to, 187–188; preparation for, 182–184; recovery from, 190–191; resources for, 194–195. *See also* Careers, post-dance; Dropouts/dropping out; Retirement

Trauma, of sexual harassment, 94–96; posttraumatic stress disorder and, 95–96; recovery from, 95–96

Travolta, J., 27

Tuff-Skin, 151

Tumkovsky, A., 35

*Turning Point, The*, 80

Turnout, basic anatomy and, 17, 152

Twelve-step programs, 135–136

Twist, 30

**U**

Unions, 119–121; resources for, 211–212

United Kingdom: career transition center, 195; medical services and clinics in, 205

United States: career transition centers in, 195–196; medical services and clinics in, 205–210

U.S. Department of Education, 94

University of Kansas, 90

University of Michigan, 50

Uprockin', 29

USA International Ballet Competition, 198

**V**

Vaganova, A., 24

Vaganova style, 24

Varna International Ballet Competition, 198

Verbal attacks, 42–44; problems caused by, 42–44

Videotapes: for auditions, 110–111; resources, 201

Virginia, medical clinic in, 210

Visualization, 137–140, 191

Vitamin supplements, 71–72

Vivid imagery, 138–139

Vocational counseling, 102, 186–187

**W**

Warm-ups, 162–163

Warren, M., 71

Washington, medical services and clinics in, 210

Water drinking, 73, 155

Watkins, A., 200

Weight, 55–62; auditions and, 113; of ballet dancers, 23, 58, 59; of ballroom dancers, 28; of dancers, 58–59, 165; dancing and losing, 57–58; diet and, 69–75; exercise and, 68–69, 73, 74–75; genetic endowment and, 56–57, 67; healthy approaches to loss/control of, 61–62, 68–75; and height, 59–60; ideal, 58; impact of, 60, 61–62; injuries and, 155, 160; of jazz dancers, 31; lifestyle change and, 74–75; of modern dancers, 25, 60; of tap dancers, 32. *See also* Anatomy; Body shape; Dieting; Eating disorders; Fat

Weight Watchers, 74

Weight-height table, 59–60

Weight-resistant exercise, 68–69

*West Side Story*, 30

*What Everyone Can Do to Fight AIDS* (Garwood and Melnick), 170, 200

Williams, J. M., 142

Wolfram, E., 211

Women. *See* Female dancers

Work habits, 38–40

**Y**

*Your Dance Résumé: A Preparatory Guide to the Audition* (Wolfram), 211

Yo-yo effect, 62